We have compassion for humanity. We see it making choices that we've made in the past and we'd like to guide you towards a better future — like an older sibling assisting a younger one.

Your world and the ideas that you've created around you exist because you believe them to. Truth exists whether you believe it or not. Truth exists beyond this world in all worlds.

Don't underestimate the power of the people to make change. Do your part — make your change — and a chain reaction will occur around you.

Ambassadors Between Worlds

Intergalactic Gateway to a New Earth

Damiana Sage Miller

New Atlantean Press
Santa Fe, New Mexico

Ambassadors Between Worlds

Intergalactic Gateway to a New Earth

ISBN: 978-1881217381

Library of Congress Cataloging-in-Publication Data

Miller, Damiana Sage, 1987-
   Ambassadors between worlds : intergalactic gateway to a new earth /
Damiana Sage Miller.
      p. cm.
Includes bibliographical references and index.
ISBN 978-1-881217-38-1 (alk. paper)
1. Human-alien encounters. 2. Consciousness--Miscellanea. I. Title.
BF2050.M57 2012
133.9'3--dc23
                              2012001972

Conversations between enlightened extraterrestrials and their ambassador
on the Earth. Topics include the nature of God, evolution of the soul, finding
your purpose, living your passion, cleaning up the environment, and developing
new energy resources.

Cover Design: NZM

Printed in the United States of America

Published by:
New Atlantean Press
PO Box 9638
Santa Fe, NM 87504
www.new-atlantean.com

*This publication is dedicated to
the conscious evolution of humanity.*

Introduction

Hello. My name is Damiana. A few months ago I had an extraordinary experience. I sat down to meditate and my third eye (the brow chakra) spontaneously awakened, allowing me to enter the world of souls. At the time that it happened, I didn't know anything about this other world. Many colorful images rapidly shot past my inner eye. They evoked uncertain feelings in me and I became overwhelmed with emotions. I couldn't focus on these images or get a clear vision; they were out of my control.

I remember seeing a woman with her child, a bridge, constellations, and many other dream-like scenes. I saw these spectacles and felt them as well. My empathy was heightened — I could feel what the people in my images were feeling. I was then overwhelmed with a burden of grief. It was too much, too quick, and I broke down sobbing. For the next twenty-four hours I had a throbbing pain directly above the bridge of my nose.

Two days later, I was serving customers food at the restaurant where I worked when I heard someone talk to me. I looked around and realized that the voice was in my head: "Welcome, being of the Light!" I had just received my first telepathic communication. I picked up my pen and transcribed the rest of the message:

> Welcome, being of the Light, welcome. You join your kindred family in a time of grand importance. Your growth and under-standing in all things divine shall expand and grow, and if you choose to continue down this path, you shall open up a Pandora's box of sorts, that is to say, the things you choose to see cannot be unseen, and they are often difficult for an emotionally-based being like yourself to observe. But we will be with you and assist you on your journey. We welcome you with great love and guidance, as we always have and always will, in lifetimes both past and future.

The message was signed by a "special friend" from my time in Atlantis.

Wow! A few days later, during one of my daily meditations, Saint Francis came through with a personal message that provided a little more insight into my newfound purpose:

> There is an internal alarm, so to speak, inside Damiana that has gone off because the world is in dire need of healers and mediums between the two worlds, several worlds actually.

Archangel Raphael had a similar message for me and other light workers:

> Welcome, Damiana. Your journey has just begun and there's so much that you can achieve if you continue down this path. It's time in your life and time on Earth for a new expansion and a new birth. A new chapter is about to begin in humanity's existence. Many light workers, like yourself, are opening up and becoming more receptive at this time. They can instinctually feel the call in their heart, because we're all connected. So, as you are starting to open up, as are others, you must banish any doubt that you might have and any negativity that you feel towards other beings, for they in their own time will awaken. But with your help and others' help, you can start fertilizing the soil for the new Earth that is brought upon us.

Some of my early channelings were meant to assure me that I wasn't imagining the internal visions and voices that I was seeing and hearing. The guides encouraged me to continue meditating and developing my third eye. I also started giving spiritual readings to family, friends, and other people who requested them. Most of the people that I do readings for live in other parts of the world. The guides know their souls and provide beneficial information, including past lives when appropriate.

Although my awakening was a surprise, in retrospect it wasn't surprising that it occurred. I had many psychic experiences growing up, several as a baby. In addition, my parents taught me how to meditate when I was a teenager. They would often receive messages from ascended masters and other beings of the Light. Although I found it interesting, I never paid much attention to it nor did I practice meditation until a few months ago.

I started meditating after seeing a video of a UFO hovering over a holy site in Jerusalem. A few weeks later, an earthquake and tsunami in Japan damaged several nuclear reactors causing radiation to spew into the atmosphere. That was deeply disturbing and caused me to turn within with even more passion and dedication; I started meditating every day. A few weeks later, my journey began.

Shortly after I had my spiritual awakening and began receiving channeled messages, my father took me on a guided meditation through a magical forest that opened up into a beautiful meadow. This is where I had my first encounter with an extraterrestrial. In fact, all of the channelings in this book are from benevolent extraterrestrials existing in other worlds. They are mainly from Pleiades, Alpha Centauri, and LaZarus (a planet located in another dimension).

All of the extraterrestrials who have communicated with me would like to help our civilization become more enlightened. There is no reason for us to fear or idolize them. Although they are technologically and spiritually advanced, they will not interfere with our free will; we must work out most of our own problems. They discuss everything from global warming and new energy resources, to karma, dharma, and evolution of the soul.

Although the Pleiadians are wise and compassionate, a lot of the information that they provide is surprising and controversial. For example, judgment is a human concept; it does not exist in higher realms. Good and evil are just labels that we give to human experiences; they don't have an objective reality. And no one ever truly dies. In fact, in some regions of the universe, souls come and go freely from their physical body to a non-physical existence.

I am lucky to have parents who support my unusual calling. We meditate together as often as possible. I continue to receive messages from several beings of Light, including benevolent extraterrestrials, angels, archangels, and ascended masters. For this book, my father asked the questions during each channeled conversation and operated the audio recorder. My mother transcribed each session. We have worked together like this during many past lives.

I hope that you will be inspired by and benefit from the channeled messages in *Ambassadors Between Worlds*. Our planet needs thoughtful, caring people who are ready to wake up, remember their true purpose on Earth, and take action raising the vibrations of humanity. Welcome to the *Intergalactic Gateway to a New Earth*.

Damiana Sage
Santa Fe, New Mexico

God is within everything, for there is the individual you and there is the collective you. And collectively, your higher Self and everyone's higher Self, makes up God.

1

Neil: Is there anyone in the meadow who would like to work with you or guide you or offer you any insight?

Damiana: Yes.

Neil: Who is there?

Damiana: An extraterrestrial.

Neil: Would he or she like to speak directly through you?

Damiana: Yes.

Neil: If you're comfortable, allow this being to do that.

Greetings. I come to you during the culmination of Earth's third-dimensional travels as you head into a new consciousness in the fourth dimension. The vibrational shift is already taking place all over your planet, consciously and unconsciously. You can think of these dimensional shifts much like the school systems of your planet, for right now you would be in third grade graduating to fourth grade. And while third grade is no lesser than fourth grade, perhaps you will learn new things and have greater freedom in fourth grade, and then again in fifth, sixth, and so on. These shifts *will* take place, no matter what.

You must understand truth, for truths are constant. But just to have a constant and not to grow from it will serve no purpose. So, learning from these truths and sharing them with others on your planet will help soften the dimensional shift.

God is within everything, for there is the individual you and there is the collective you. And collectively, *your* higher Self and *everyone's* higher Self, makes up God.

The universe, constantly expanding, will eventually boomerang back, and it will all start over again.

We care for the humans, for we were where you are now, much like a fifth grader giving advice to a third grader.

Do you have any questions?

Yes. Who are you and where are you from?

You can call me Naor. I am from a planetary system just north of Orion, called LaZarus. We are friends with the Pleiadians, the Essassani, and the Sirius, but we are our own species.

What are your main reasons for being here on the Earth, or near the Earth, at this time?

We are here to guide and watch over you and make sure your paradigm shift goes over smoother, to teach those who will listen, and to make change upon your planet so you can join us in higher dimensions.

Do you travel by ship or do you have some other means of arriving here?

We do have ships, but I am speaking to you telepathically. Telepathy and empathy are two and the same, and Damiana is a fine vessel to speak through.

Do you see Damiana working with your group more often or will she be working with different groups? How do you see that unfolding?

That will be up to Damiana. But, yes, we would love to work with her, as would many different extraterrestrials and spirits. She is still at the very beginning stages, but we see her coming along just fine.

What advice do you have for humans in general to help us move forward with the shift? Do you see any serious Earth changes, more pain and destruction that we as a civilization are going to have to contend with?

Yes, there will be many Earth changes but fear and pain are low forms of vibration. It's important to understand those forms and rise above them. Joy, ecstasy and knowledge are all higher forms of vibration, and those shall help you through the shifts. So, living *your* life with joy and purpose will help *you* through the shift, and you, in turn, can help others.

When we say you are graduating from the third dimension to the fourth, realize that this will actually occur in a longer period than you perceive. There shall be many Earth changes upcoming within the next 100, 200, 300 years. But you must live in the Now because that is all you have — Now — and the stages of the shift are already happening, but it will take many years for it to be complete. The Earth will continue to have earthquakes, volcanoes and tsunamis, and the atmosphere has become depleted. But it will rejuvenate itself, and what you see as Earth right now in the third dimension will be a different planet in the fourth dimension.

How serious is global warming and do we have a problem with CO_2 in our atmosphere?

Absolutely. Unfortunately, Earth is extremely contaminated. It really is at a point — I don't want to say of no return — but it is at a tipping point, and it really is important for the beings of Earth to discover other energy fields. There are many energetic, magnetic fields emitting from the Earth that could be very beneficial to you if you learn how to use them. And solar power, which you have already harnessed in some ways, can be used in so many more. Your own vibrational fields — as well as all things existing anywhere, everywhere — also have their own energy that can be harnessed.

Will extraterrestrials be providing us with technology or guidance on cleaning up our atmosphere or do we need to do this on our own?

We have provided several of your leaders with help, with guidance, with technology. How they choose, and have chosen, to use it is beyond our help. But we will work with those who ask and try to make your Earth more livable.

Well, thank you. This has been a real treat communicating with you. Do you have anything else you'd like to share with us at this time?

I will be back. Thank you for letting me come through. I hope you have a wonderful day.

You must constantly work at non-attachment — non-attachment of possessions, of ideas, of negative energy — for Earth is just an experience that will pass and the eternal Now will be ever present.

2

Hello. We welcome you as ambassadors building bridges between different worlds in different dimensions. You should take this job with pride and honor and continue training yourselves to be the most pure, kindred vessels in which to transmit this information. You must constantly keep in mind what your purpose is, and intent, always working towards your higher Selves, constantly being aware of your internal agreement and soul purpose, working towards pure enlightenment.

The being, which is you, is made up of a Holy Trinity: the soul, the mind, and the body. All three must be working at maximum energy and highest vibrations, for when one is off kilter it creates an imbalance.

You must constantly work at non-attachment — non-attachment of possessions, of ideas, of negative energy — for Earth is just an experience that will pass and the eternal Now will be ever present. So continue living your life working towards complete wholeness, complete love, complete Godliness, but realize that several of the negative experiences on your planet, too, shall pass.

Souls, like yourselves, make the choice to reincarnate to experience all that mortal life has to offer. And while on a higher plane you have greater understanding and see the whole picture, it's all conceptual; to experience it, you must live it. The soul yearns for these experiences.

You must always feel and be aware of your constant connection to God, for She/He is always with you.

You must try to let go of passing judgments, for every being is doing just that — being. They will find their path on their own or karmically.

May I answer any questions for you?

Well, first of all, who are you and where are you from?

15

I am an extraterrestrial; you may call me Adam. I am from Pleiades and constantly watching over your planet.

How did you come to speak through Damiana this day?

Damiana and I are connected telepathically right now. She is feeling what I feel and creating meaning behind it.

Are you a distinct being from other Pleiadians? Why are *you* speaking through today rather than, for example, any other Pleiadian or any other extraterrestrial or spiritual being?

There are so many Pleiadians, other extraterrestrials, beings of Light, guides, masters — so many eager to connect. I just so happen to be the one who made the connection today. I can continue visiting in the future or others can come through too. In the future, you can ask for us by name or by feeling if you would like to speak with a particular entity.

At this time, our main goal is to work with Damiana so that she can become a better vessel for communication. Do you have any guidance to offer or anything to say about that?

Damiana has a natural gift, but like any talent she must continue to work at it. Discipline within her meditations, and intent — not only in her meditations, but always — will help train her into becoming a more direct channel.

Is this something Damiana has developed over past lives.

Oh, yes. Damiana has always been an ambassador between different worlds, often from the other side guiding earthly and other-planet beings. This life, she's chosen to experience back on Earth and she will continue to bring forth her gift.

Damiana wants to know why we forget our purpose when we come to the Earth. Why do we seem to have a veil over our awareness?

Free will is one of the few non-limitations you are given on Earth. It's one of the many experiences that being human offers, and to fully enjoy and fully experience the many different choices that being human offers it's often in your best interest to go forth somewhat blindly. However, especially as a child, most humans *do* remember a purpose. You can ask any child what they want to do; most of them have a direct answer. Unfortunately, choices, influences, and different experiences throughout life can bury or alter the original intent.

Damiana was always interested in theater but now it seems obvious that channeling is her gift and purpose — to be an ambassador between worlds. Can you tell us why she had such an interest in theater?

Yes, Damiana has always enjoyed the performance aspect of theater. However, her first instincts were towards artistic abilities, and that gift is inspired and channeled from her higher Self. Channeling has always been part of Damiana's vibrations. It was important for her to experience different avenues to add to her understanding of what this planet has to offer. We knew that she would eventually wander down this path, for it isn't by accident that she chose you and Susanne as her parents.

Damiana wants to know why humans have disease.

Dis-ease is caused from emotional strain on the soul, which is then brought forth on the physical body. Unfortunately, most disease is brought on karmically from past lives, future lives, and often your present life. When you send out negative vibrations, you're really causing dis-ease in yourself. There are cures for all of the diseases, but unfortunately certain beings on your planet prefer to profit from dis-ease instead of helping other beings. However, that is their karmic path and you should not feel anger towards them.

Will Damiana be able to receive healing advice from the guides similar to what Edgar Cayce provided to help others?

With lots of training and discipline, the possibilities are endless. Damiana truly does have a wonderful gift, as do all souls. However, Damiana is on the path towards the greater good and, yes, we can see that being part of her purpose.

You mentioned earlier that humans are made up of a Holy Trinity of the body, mind, and soul. How do the mind and soul differ?

Beings on your planet have lots of names for these: the id, the ego, the superego; the conscious, the subconscious, the superconscious. All of these are referring to the Holy Trinity: the Father, the Son, the Holy Ghost. The soul and the mind will leave the body when it is time. The soul is everything you are and everything there is. Your soul is your higher Self connected to God. Your mind is your memory, thoughts, actions, intent. Together, they achieve divinity. Your earthly body holds them and keeps them safe, and in turn you must keep it safe.

Does everyone have a predestined length of life? Is that dictated by genetics? How does that work?

Yes and no. You always have choices. If you are no longer content, you're always free to move on. However, you do not want to live — your soul does not want to continue on — in a body that has grown brittle and weak. It knows that together the body and soul have an agreement when it is time to move on. It is better for the soul to reincarnate into a young, more able body than continue in a body past its prime.

Today, there are many people with bodies that are broken down. For example, many children have autism and they seem to have certain physical limitations. Would you speak about this?

Yes. This is a combination of karmic limitations as well as beings on your planet who consciously know how to protect babies and children from these limitations, but choose not to. Unfortunately, greed, pride and power are very influential in many beings' lives. You must realize that they are not important in your life; you will be taken care of when you live your life with love, peace, understanding, joy and purpose.

Is suffering karmic?

In some cases, but not all of them. Suffering is a human condition that has been put in place for thousands of years to give human beings a chance to experience compassion and to put compassion into action by making the choice to end it. The soul constantly yearns for experiences. Although it is all-knowing, this knowingness is conceptual, so to truly understand any situation the soul must live and walk in its own shoes. For example, try explaining an orgasm. You have an idea in your head and you can explain what goes on biologically, but you can't truly understand it without experiencing it. The soul constantly wants to feel all different experiences, even ones that are perhaps painful or scary, but it then gives you the opportunity to improve. This is the case most often with disabled beings. Before they entered the body, they mapped out a plan of their life; they chose to experience these impairments (for example, being blind, deaf or handicapped). This is their choice and often has nothing to do with karma. There is an exception to this. It has to do with the free will of other beings inflicted on them, for example a mother who drinks alcohol or does drugs while pregnant or in a car accident. Souls must then adjust to these challenges inflicted on them and make the best choices that they can.

Thank you for coming through today. I really enjoyed this conversation with you. We send many blessings over to your side, as we know that you send blessings to us.

Thank you. Have a blessed day.

Karma is a universal law; it will manifest itself no matter where you reincarnate yourself. There comes a point, however, when you step outside the Karmic Ring and are on a path of pure service and enlightenment.

3

Good afternoon. It is I, Adam, your friend from Pleiades. I come to you today knowing that the state in which you reside is going up in flames, so to speak. [At the time of this channeling, New Mexico had several large forest fires.] We are not happy to see this happening, for it is a direct result of the depletion of your atmosphere causing temperatures to skyrocket making it much easier for your world to become like a matchstick box. But do not let it stifle your creative energy, for this too shall pass, and like the Phoenix coming from the flames, the Earth will rise above it. Sharing your gifts and your energy shall help release some of your creative vibrations into the atmosphere and into the universe and help raise the vibrations and the consciousness of the planet, for they *do* affect other beings whether they know it or not. May I answer any questions today?

I have some philosophical questions. Why do so many people on the Earth seem lost?

You set up a society that has created standards, layers, classes, and monetary systems. Many beings come to this planet with high ideals but often the need to survive takes over. Greed and power drive some souls toward negative energy. However, do not think all souls are lost, for many souls are just trying different experiences that the Earth has to offer, so you may look at a homeless being who has become addicted to substances or you may look at someone who has let money control their life and they seem lost to you, but perhaps they have chosen to experience the darker sides of their nature as a soul or they've chosen to experience compassion and empathy through how others respond to them. You must remember the saying that your planet has: "Not all those who wander are lost." Many are just on their own path, experiencing the many different paths that there are.

This brings up another question that Damiana and I were discussing the other day. We don't want to judge other people; we want to be non-judgmental and yet we have to be discerning. Sometimes we might see people and think, "I don't want that person in my life or influencing me." How do we resolve the apparent discrepancy between remaining non-judgmental and having to make wise choices in our life?

Yes, it's very important to *discern* between discernment and judgment, for being a human being gives you free will. It is important that you execute that free will by making proper choices for your life, well-being, and the path that you have to take. However, it is not your place to have negative or unsavory thoughts toward other beings. As I said, they're on their own path, but it is your choice if you do not want certain beings in your life or if you don't want to make the same choices as those beings. But understanding them, realizing why those beings are that way or why they're making those choices — and not letting it affect you, positively or negatively — is in your best interest.

I understand that we have free will on the Earth when we as souls take up residence for a period of time inside the physical body. Do other beings elsewhere have free will, and if not, what is that experience like?

Many beings elsewhere are very similar to humans, and many experiences on other planets are very similar to your own. There are many other planets in the universe that look and seem nearly identical to the Earth and, yes, beings on these planets also have free will as do many other beings, many extraterrestrials. Free will is one of the few non-limitations of Earth, and as you raise your vibration and enter into other dimensions, your free will will not be lost, but more will be gained as far as limitations go. What you are thinking of as *not* free will is an all-knowingness that some beings have and making proper choices to assist in the development of other beings and other souls. However, I would not say that they do not have free will. They do have free will, but they choose to execute their choices in a certain direction. Does that make sense?

Yes, I think so. It seems like an expanded will, as though free will increases to where these beings are only doing that which is in the best interest of others or of the whole.

Yes, indeed.

Are we talking about beings like angels and ascended masters?

Yes, correct. Both angels and ascended masters.

Perhaps you can offer a little bit of insight into a complicated topic. Many of us on the Earth are grappling with the concept of time. To us it seems linear. Here on the Earth we have a past, we have a present, and we imagine that we have a future. Yet, sometimes we hear that time is happening all at once or that all of our past lives did not really happen in the past but that they're really happening in the ever present Now. These are very difficult concepts for us to wrap our minds around. Can you speak about this for a moment?

Yes. You must live in the Now for truly that is what you have, and for this life on Earth, time will seem linear. You set it up that way; this is one of the many limitations that Earth has to offer. Time is the fourth dimension and as you move forward from the third to the fourth, many of these concepts will become clearer. But right now it is beyond your comprehension in a lot of ways. If you had never heard music or tasted food, how would you be able to describe that? It would be beyond your comprehension, and at this point in time, time is like that. But it is important to understand that it is all of what you said and much more; there is a past, there is a future, and yet it is all happening right now. It's important to focus on the Now. Always focus on the Now.

Why is that important? Why does focusing on the Now seem to take precedence?

Because the Now is truly all there is, for the past is gone and the future will come — but when it comes it will be the Now. It's important to live in the moment and live for what's happening at this particular time. It is important to learn and grow from the past and look forward to the future, but you'll lose grasp of the importance taking place right now if you're constantly looking to the past and the future.

Thank you. Do you have anything else to share with us before we end today's session?

Continue making time for the meditations and the channeling. The level you wish to reach will be achieved. Please be patient. Many blessings from our side to yours. Always love and light in your world. We wish you a wonderful day.

4

Greetings. It is I, Naor. How are you today?

Good, thank you.

Beings from my planet eagerly await the universal enlightenment that has begun on your planet, for we are all connected; when the vibrations are raised on your planet, they are sent out and connected with our vibrations. The shift has already begun and we are eager and excited for you.

May I answer any questions today?

I have a question that I think a lot of people wonder about. Perhaps you can offer some insight into the differences between angels, archangels, ascended masters, and extraterrestrials. It's difficult for us to understand the differences and whether different classifications of beings truly exist.

There are many beings of Light, much like different animal species. When souls reach a certain level of enlightenment after many years of service, they can achieve ascended master status. This includes souls having the human experience, souls having the extraterrestrial experience, or souls just living on the astral plane. Archangels can also be ascended masters. They are angels that have gone above and beyond in service and achieved a higher rank of enlightenment.

Angels work directly with the Source providing guidance for souls on many different levels on many different worlds. They protect and watch over you. We, extraterrestrials, are like you, human beings, just having experiences on a different planet. We, too, are working towards enlightenment and we, too, have many souls that have reached ascension. Does that make sense?

Yes, thank you. I want to talk about time once again. Time, of course, is a very difficult concept for us to grasp. I would like to know how extra-

terrestrials monitor the Earth. How do you know what's actually taking place on the Earth? Do you have spaceships that are in our atmosphere? According to Albert Einstein's Theory of Relativity, nothing can travel faster than the speed of light, so how do you get here from such great distances? Can you explain some of this?

Yes. Many extraterrestrials are living within your view of the galaxy, just in another dimension. So, we can monitor your Earth activity without being detected, much like you watching someone from a two-way mirror. The extraterrestrials are with you, but you can't see them. In many instances, however, extraterrestrials will come from far away. Our technology is extremely advanced and we can travel instantly — much faster than the speed of light.

Some extraterrestrials can fold time and space. If you think of the universe as a net horizontally spread out with different points in time existing on different points of the net, and if you're at point A and you want to get to point B, certain technology allows for the folding of this net allowing the two times to coincide, where they're more or less in two places simultaneously. This also speaks on a theory of time happening all at once, for it is possible to continue folding time and space.

Time is a concept that is very difficult to grasp, but as you move towards the fourth dimension it will become easier. Earth beings, too, will eventually space travel, for many of the technologies that you have on your planet were gifts from extraterrestrials — and many of your secret governments are already working on spacecraft that have our technology.

How were they able to acquire this technology and why isn't it shared with the masses?

Many secret governments meet regularly with different beings of space — some positive influences and some negative. For example, for many years an extraterrestrial race known as the Grays has been doing trades — and their technology is some of the most advanced in the universe — in exchange for cover-ups of abductions. There will come a time when this technology is brought to the masses, but right now these secret governments continue to keep you in the dark covering up any alien interaction as a conspiracy theory, but this will come to light.

Do you agree that if everyone today became aware of the truth about the existence of extraterrestrials that it would disrupt our economic, religious, and cultural systems?

Yes and no. There are already quite a few beings on your planet who are becoming aware of our existence, as we are slowly coming to you in small doses. We would not like to overwhelm your planet, for human beings throughout history have looked upon newcomers with fear or greed, and we would not like to be attacked or abused. But we will continue making our presence known more and more; eventually there will be a connection that will be known worldwide.

I spoke to a physicist and asked him about your idea of accessing energy from the magnetic fields of the Earth. He said that the Earth's magnetic fields are very weak and that our current technology won't allow us to do that; it's not a viable option to acquire energy from that source. Can you speak about this?

Yes. What he is referring to as "weak" is only *subtle* and these subtle energies can be harnessed. The beings on your planet often look for the strongest, the best, the most abundant. But when you look for subtle, influential, small energies that can be used, they can be of the utmost benefit to your society. These energies have been used throughout time. Atlantis utilized Earth's magnetic fields. They were able to build structures with these energies without lifting a finger. When you harness and connect *your* magnetic field, *your* energy, into these subtle Earth energies, you can create a link with the utmost power.

I do not believe that you are ready right now — that your planet is ready right now — to harness these energies, for every being could tap into this and you would not be able to profit from it. So, until your planet is ready to set aside monetary gain and is ready to look for alternative energy sources because your beings finally realize they are destroying their world, it won't be time to tap into these resources.

I'm guessing that when you travel great distances from other star systems and come to our solar system you would employ this technology that folds time or folds the universe, but that once you're here in our solar system or in the Earth's atmosphere with your craft you would then employ a different system of mobility, perhaps using electromagnetic fields. Am I correct that a different system is employed once you're here?

We, the LaZari, are within your solar system already, just a different dimension. And while many of us explore the universe, most of us reside close to our planet or near other ones within your galaxy. We do use craft that have instantaneous — so it would seem instantaneous — technology that is faster than the speed of light. We have tapped into our own energy sources as well as the constant energy that exists within everything around us. We utilize our energy along with energy of the desired location and transport immediately to where we want to go.

Is this associated with quantum mechanics? I understand that twin particles can have instantaneous rapport that seems to be out of the domain of Albert Einstein's Theory of Relativity which limits space travel to the speed of light. Can you speak about that?

Yes. Where many of the quantum physicists are going with the twin particles is how we transport. However, we also utilize these energy sources we've been talking about. So, many of the beings on your planet are headed in the right direction learning many mysteries of the universe in different ways.

Is your technology 300 years advanced, 1,000 years advanced, or 10,000 years advanced when compared to Earth technology? How would you describe the differences?

These technologies could become available to your planet within the next 100 years if you choose to raise your consciousness and accept the many, many different beings that are in your universe. You could have many different technologies that exist for advanced alien civilizations. However, we do not see this necessarily happening, so our technology may be 500 or so years advanced, but it is possible that it could happen much sooner.

If we were able to visit your civilization, would we recognize it as a physical world? Can you show yourself as a physical entity or are you a higher dimensional being, one that we would never be able to see physically?

I am both. I am a fifth-dimensional being but I do have a physical existence. I can separate myself from my physical body whenever I choose, or return to it. We have a planet much like yours, although it is much more natural. We utilize the energy that comes from it. We idolize the plants and animals that exist on our planet. We do not have houses or buildings like you do. We do have craft that surround our planet with different technologies and varied pursuits, for like you we have beings with purpose who do art, who do science, who play games, and who enjoy each other's company. Many of them travel through space. Many of them stay on our planet and mind-travel, like I am now. One day, we will meet in physical body or in non-physical soul.

How do you procreate?

We have sexual organs like you do, we enjoy sex like you do, and we have children like you do.

Is your DNA similar to ours?

In some ways we are alike, but in many ways we're different. We're short, compared to your world — around three or four feet tall. We have hair on our heads like you do, small upturned eyes, and ears. Our skin is much thicker than yours, similar to your leather. We wear robes like your Japanese kimonos, made of very thin material similar to your silk.

Do you breathe oxygen?

We breathe oxygen on our planet, but we have also found ways to breathe when we are out space traveling.

Do you have anything else that you'd like to share with us today before we end this session?

I would like to continue working with Damiana and yourself, for your planet is on an upward climb right now and we would very much like to assist you. We have lots of compassion for the human race and we would like to see you reach a place of enlightenment because, like I said, we are all connected. With your growth we achieve growth as well; we're all heading upwards together.

I will be back soon. Many blessings, with love and light.

5

Greetings, I am Aurora from Alpha Centauri, one of your protectors of the Earth. We work with the Pleiadians making sure that no harm from outside sources affects your planet. Unfortunately, we cannot protect the Earth from its own inhabitants, for we must honor the free will of souls making choices, experiencing different lives on Earth and the cleaning of their karmic slate. One day, on a different plane we will speak again in different form, but until then I would very much like to continue working with you, for we would like to help guide the Earth towards a more enlightened, safe living environment.

May I answer any of your questions today?

Yes. What exactly are your responsibilities? How do the objectives of Alpha Centaurians differ from commitments made by other benevolent beings who are working with humanity?

Although we are extraterrestrial in form, we do work with ascended masters, angels and archangels. We are all working towards the greater good. We took it upon ourselves to be one of your many protectors. Unfortunately, not all extraterrestrials believe in the uplifting of humanity; some of them wish for your demise. We will not let this happen. We are at the front lines, so to speak, making sure that Earth stays *protected*. We also work with benevolent beings towards the *enlightenment* of humanity. We would like to see the humans join us in this understanding of universal, divine enlightenment.

Which extraterrestrials are dangerous to humanity? What benefit would they gain by ending our existence?

Some beings such as the Reptilians don't want you *not* to exist, so to speak, but they would very much like to enslave you, and you would make a tasty snack for them, unfortunately.

Other beings, similar to the Reptilians, also have this idea in their head. They are a purely carnivorous and cannibalistic race, and if we weren't as strong and spiritually aware as we are, we too would be in their line of attack. However, because of our strength and awareness they are unable to come anywhere near us. You, too, will achieve this one day, for when you are on the spiritual plane, you are strong and protected.

Where does God fit into this? What does God have to say about any of this?

God is everything. You are God. I am God. The Reptilians are God. We are all One in this universe. God is the eternal love source. He is everything that is good in the world. However, to truly understand good and understand love there must be polarities. Yet, they are just experiences; _you_ put the label on them.

How long have you been Earth's protector?

We have been protecting the Earth since its inception. During the Atlantean and Lemurian stages and other beginning civilizations, we interacted face-to-face with human beings as they accepted us without fear. We are encouraged and excited to think that there will once again be a time when we can speak face-to-face. But, until then we will continue in this manner.

How far back does time go? Please talk about the Big Bang. Did it really occur?

Yes and no. Everything started at one point, but at the same time, time is not really linear. Time just is, and it continues backward and forward, almost in a ring. So, there is no beginning and there is no end. In your perception, yes, at one point it just began. Everything was and everything began after that: a universe just shot out, is continuing to expand, and at one point will bounce back into itself. However, it's all happening at the same time. It's beginning, it's ending, it's all at the same time. I know this is very hard to conceive, but as you humans move into the fourth dimension this concept of time will be more understood, as it is a constant.

If time is the fourth dimension and some extraterrestrials exist in the fifth dimension, what exactly does this mean? That's especially difficult for us to comprehend.

Yes, it's very difficult to comprehend. These dimensions are all around you all the time. They already exist. Your vibrations, however, are at a different level. So, when you raise your vibrations to these levels, you can experience these different dimensions. For example, sound is a vibration that is constantly vibrating around you, only it has to be at a certain wavelength for you to hear it. But there are sounds all around that perhaps your animals can hear, but you cannot at this time. You have to get more in tune to hear them, and then there are even sounds that your animals at this time cannot hear, and it just continues. Everything that is, is made up of vibrations. Everything you've created in your world is different wavelengths. You are different wavelengths, so like a string on a guitar, you can pluck one in a certain wavelength and pluck another for a higher wavelength. Humans — or beings of all types — can work on raising their vibrations to a higher wavelength. However, it will take a global vibrational shift to move you into a higher dimension, although it does happen naturally over your concept of time.

What are some of the most important non-physical laws and how do they operate?

There are several laws. There is the *Law of Attraction*, or Manifestation, as you might say — what you put out you shall get back. However, this law only operates through non-attachment, for when you are too connected to an idea or a concept it lingers and cannot be brought back. So, it's important to know exactly what you want in your life, put it out, work towards it, but not be attached to it.

There is also the *Law of Karma*. This operates on several different levels. Like the previous law, what you wish to receive back is related to what you put out.

The *Law of Dharma* — having a purpose and working towards enlightenment.

The _Law of Within_ — as within, so without, for what is within you will be manifested in the world about you.

These four are the most common and most important. They operate on all planes in all worlds in all dimensions.

Do we really have lessons to learn?

That is truly up to the individual soul, for you choose to come back. You choose to put out negative energy and receive negative energy back; so too with the positive. These lessons that you learn are just experiences. The soul is constantly yearning for experience and so you learn: "I do not kill people; this is not a good experience." And the lesson is then truly learned when you experience suffering in a subsequent life.

What is consciousness?

Consciousness is part of the Holy Trinity — your body, mind and soul. Consciousness is part of your mind. It continues after death and is carried on into the second life, third life, future lives. Some souls are more conscious than others, while others will get there eventually.

What is the purpose of animals in our lives?

Animals have always been very connected with spirit. Many beings can experience compassion and love through animals. We also have animals on our planet, and I personally don't think I could enjoy my form and time on this planet as much if I could not experience the love and compassion that animals provide. They have many lessons to teach us about instincts, love and nature, for they live the simplest of understandings that some humans have yet to grasp.

What is the relationship of numbers and mathematics to reality?

Mathematics reveals patterns seen throughout the universe. It connects a universal code that can be unlocked, for everything in nature, in your world, in our world, in the universe, can be related and connected through numbers and patterns. Although you've given them names and symbols, numbers and mathematics truly reveal a pattern, and everything in the universe has a pattern that can be connected. There are many tools that can help you, much like Astrology, or even Astronomy, and when you unlock these patterns it can help your understanding of the universe.

How does Astrology work?

Astrology, like numbers, works in patterns, and your connection with everything that is can be seen through astrology. When you as a soul first enter upon the Earth plane, you are immediately connected with different planets, with different stars — with everything in the universe — and these show links between personalities, ways of life, ideas, concepts. Actually, you are at the very beginning stages of understanding all there is to know about astrology, for right now you are only linked within your solar system, within your dimension. However, you are truly connected with everything in the universe, and this will become clearer as your vibrations are raised into further dimensions.

Can you provide a key to something unique about astrology that will help astrologers improve their ability to interpret charts and help people?

Perhaps astrologers should take into consideration karma and a soul's choice, why they connected at that time with that point in the universe. That can help move it along a bit. Also, for some souls the point of conception has importance on their astrological chart.

What are dreams and what is the best way to interpret them?

Dreams are very important. They allow all beings on your planet to connect with the astral plane, for they are your experience on the astral plane. You can do anything you like on the astral plane. It is the same experience as after death or before birth. Dreams are what you create them to be, and sometimes your higher Self will show you past or future lives to give you guidance in this life. Dreams are tools that will interject symbols, concepts and ideas to help you in this lifetime. It is very beneficial for humanity to pay more attention to their dreams, because like entering the world from other dimensions, you often forget them.

Is the astral world a place that we want to experience or is it a place that we should try to avoid?

You have experienced the astral world. It's a very freeing experience and, yes, you should be excited when your time comes. But until then, continue to work with a purpose to help humanity, to help clean your karmic slate, until you're ready to go back to the love, compassion, and understanding found on the astral plane. There were times when you could easily go between both worlds; the body was not so trapping.

I think of the astral plane as a world of emotional desires, something that we need to gain control over. Perhaps you have a different definition.

The astral world is just the world for souls. It is the afterlife and the before-life. You can make choices there and see the whole picture. It is very freeing. I would not call it emotional, per se. It is very understanding, for it is nonjudgmental and takes in all souls, no matter what the life experience was, good or bad.

How do you see your relationship with Damiana — and hers with other extraterrestrials — unfolding? What are your plans? How do you see your group, the Alpha Centauri, working with her in the future?

We (myself, as well as other benevolent extraterrestrials) would like to continue working through Damiana as ambassadors from our planet, hopefully spreading words of wisdom and encouragement to many beings of your planet so they can move forward into higher dimensions and continue towards a more enlightened civilization. So, perhaps we can speak through Damiana to many, many Earth beings.

Thank you for coming through and communicating with us. Do you have anything else you'd like to say before we end our session?

Thank you for letting me in today. I do appreciate it. I will be back. Many blessings.

6

Good afternoon. It is I, Naor, your dear friend from LaZarus. How are you on this fine afternoon?

We're doing great, thank you.

Good to hear it. I'm very happy to be joining you once again, making these intergalactic communications. We find it very exciting and uplifting to see that some of our sessions are now being shared online. Hopefully, they will be read without fear and not taken too seriously, for that is not our intent. We all make our own reality. So, while I may be very real in your heads, perhaps I do not exist in everyone else's. But we do look forward to seeing how we are perceived.

May I answer any questions today?

Please discuss the crop circle phenomenon. What is that all about?

While the crop circles are not part of our culture, many other extraterrestrials enjoy a little folly and game, teasing the humans. However, many of the crop circles are messages and reminders to humans that you were once friends with extra-terrestrials. We walked among you upon the Earth and you did not fear us. Please try to remember.

The crop circles are formed using vibrations, much like everything in the universe. Many of them are codes and symbols of communication. Some of them are just beautiful works of art. Extraterrestrials will continue leaving hints of their existence through UFO sightings, crop circles, and telepathic communications like this one.

Do you have any clues for us regarding how to interpret or decipher these crop circles?

Many of the crop circles are not meant to be deciphered. Instead, they are to remind you of your friendly space brothers. Some of them are codes and tools and patterns that together can create incredible technology. However, until you recognize the connection that you have with the entire universe, they shall remain mysteries.

I read about an extraterrestrial group known as Lyricus. Can you comment on them?

Lyricus is an extraterrestrial civilization from many, many years ago (by your understanding of time). They, too, worked with ancient human civilizations and they still work with those who will listen. There are so many extraterrestrial civilizations in this infinite universe existing in different dimensions and different times. You can communicate with many of them who wish to speak to you through telepathy, like we are doing now.

Damiana is having a little trouble today, so we are going to take a moment to reconnect...

Can you hear me now? How about now? Is the reception better? I bet you didn't know that we, too, have a sense of humor. May I answer anything else for you?

(Smiles) Yes. Please speak about some of the different extraterrestrial groups that are working directly with humanity today, especially the ones that wish to guide and enlighten us. Also tell us about some of the extraterrestrial groups that are working with humanity for different reasons.

Absolutely. There are we, the LaZari, although this is quite new to us as well. I don't believe that too many human beings know us that well yet, but they will. There are our benevolent friends the Pleiadians, who have worked with you throughout time; the Alpha Centauri, your protectors; the Sirians; the Essassani. There is another group that communicates through clicking, much like some of your native African cultures. We will just call them Civilization X right now. There are also the Kryons who will communicate occasionally and are benevolent. And there are many space travelers who come and make connections individually.

The Reptilians are not your friends, although there are occasionally rogue vegetarian Reptilians who go against their culture and have soft spots for humanity. The Grays have always been linked with your society, and while their intentions are not to harm you, mutual agreements between the Grays and your government are more in the Grays' favor.

A lot of people are interested in the Bible. I regard many of the Bible stories as true accounts of historical events. Some of the others seem mythical, such as the stories of Creation or Adam and Eve and the Garden of Eden. Would you speak about the Bible?

Yes. The Bible tells wonderful stories. While some are historical accounts, many are stories. As for the beginning of time, time at that time was not recorded and divided into segments as it is on your planet today. What was recorded as seven days was actually, as you know time, hundreds of thousands of years. As for Adam and Eve, they were not the first beings on your planet. They did exist, however, and were connected spiritually with the Creator. There were several civilizations and developments over time but they did not understand or remember the lifetimes before them, so they thought they were the first. While many aspects of the Bible make good guidelines for living, it's important for humanity not to be attached to any idea or take any of it too literally, as many of the beings on your planet do. However, I'm sure they shall consider me blasphemous for saying so.

What is the spiritual connection of the Jewish people to the planet and why do they seem to be especially persecuted?

The Jews are not the only "chosen people" — all people are "chosen." They, like all souls, are on their karmic journey and have had many points of karmic responsibility. Although it seems like their karma isn't quite clean yet, it is on its way, while many other beings are also cleaning their karmic slates.

What do you see regarding Israel and the Middle East? What can be done by either side to make that relationship more peaceful?

Unfortunately, Palestine is not anywhere close to a compromise and it would take the raising of the white flag from either side. We do not see this happening anytime soon. However, that doesn't mean that something couldn't change very rapidly.

What is it that your group from LaZarus would like to teach humanity? If you're going to continue speaking through Damiana in the future, do you have any special interests or topics that you would like to discuss?

We would love to teach on many topics, from the power of thought and manifestation, to karmic law, to love, to peace, to enlightenment, to more everyday topics, like attracting a partner and a career, as well as how to create the life you want and realize that life is just a stage — there is so much more afterwards — and how you can be best at service to humanity to assist in the enlightening of the masses and help your community go forth in a more civilized and regal manner.

Do you see yourself talking on specific topics for a period of time or do you prefer answering questions on a multitude of topics?

We can do it either way. We are always interested to see what you would like to know. So, perhaps we can do both.

Yes, because we're not only interested in our own questions that we'd like answered, but we'd also like to hear what you think is important for us to know.

Perhaps in the future we can divide our time between the two. I can start off with a teaching, so to speak, and then open the floor up to questions.

That sounds like a good plan.

All right, it is agreed upon.

Do you have anything else that you'd like to share with us before we end today's session?

Many blessings. I bid you good day.

7

We have encircled the Earth in a beautiful, protective golden ring. It is time for Earthlings to practice non-attachment, for they are much too attached to the third dimension and the silly, mundane culture they have created for themselves. Limitations have been accepted without question because they do not all realize or remember where they came from or where they are going. It's time to remove themselves from these limitations, to detach from the social norm and all things that their civilization has set forth to control them.

Don't you think that the "human being" experience has gone on long enough? Isn't it time to experience the pure, divine, unaltered spiritual beings that you all are? You are all part of the Source. You are all demigods. You make the reality that you see, and while the truth is a constant, reality is not. Everyone has their own idea of what is real. Can all be right? Can their truth be different from your truth and yet somehow still be truth?

Trace minerals that exist on the Earth's surface are creating connections with the plants, animals, and human beings. They contain extraterrestrial energy that is being projected into your world, affecting and awakening several beings. Never stop questioning your world, for those who ask shall find answers.

As we look into your future, we see so much of the past. It is up to you to change that so as not to repeat it.

May I answer any questions for you?

Who are you?

My name is Ponna; I am from Pleiades.

Are you speaking with Damiana telepathically right now?

Yes, indeed I am.

Please elaborate on the trace minerals on the surface of the Earth.

There are many minerals that we, the Pleiadians, have dropped there many moons ago. They hold secrets, interacting with you every day, even in your sleep, giving warnings and reminders and awakening some souls who otherwise would not be aware of the times now needing change. These minerals exist within your soil, sands, and clays.

Are these like vitamins that we can ingest? Can we rub them on our bodies? Can scientists dissect and extract energy from them?

They are not meant to be dissected. But, yes, you can gain energy from them by rubbing them on your body, making mud baths with clay, or burying yourself in sand the next time you go to the beach. However, these minerals interact with you either way, without direct contact. They are all about you, coating your land and extending around the Earth's surface.

Do you continue adding minerals to the Earth or were they placed here a long time ago and still prevalent today?

At this time we are not adding any minerals. We coated the Earth with them thousands of years ago. The energy from them is still very strong and growing by the day.

Why did you mention these minerals? What benefit can we gain from knowing about them? As a human species, we still have problems making peace and living in an enlightened fashion within our culture, so it doesn't seem like the minerals have had much of a positive effect in that regard.

The minerals are not going to bring global peace. They are only reminders and encouragement to awaken some beings who would not otherwise be awoken. They emit positive energy into your everyday life. We mention these minerals because they are just starting to take effect and we think it is important for you to be aware of the connection you will have with them. We also mention them to let you know that while we are not going to step in to control your free will, we are proactive in assisting your planet in many ways.

Do these minerals have names?

They are not common ones like you know. We created these minerals from pure thought thousands of years ago.

You mentioned something about the difference between truth and reality. Could you elaborate on that?

Is there a difference between truth and reality? That is quite a question to ponder, isn't it? Truth is an absolute while reality is what you have created. Reality can sometimes align with truth. However, it can also stand alone and not be real but a creation of one's own imagination. Does that make it any less real, though? I don't believe it does.

Do you have anything else that you'd like to share with us before we end today's session?

I would very much like to thank you for letting me come through and let you know how much we appreciate human beings. We truly wish to see you succeed in moving your planet to a positive, civilized understanding of the universe.

Many blessings from our side to yours. With love and light, I bid you good day.

Several things are just being. They don't exist in any past or present form. They are just existing — as is God, your higher Self, time, love, and karma. They are all constants. They are not going anywhere. They are not coming from anywhere. They just are. They always will be.

8

Today we shall begin our session by talking about good and evil, or the labels that humanity has given to different experiences, for do good and evil truly exist in the scope of the universe? It seems that you cannot have one without the other, and that in order to experience and know what good is, you must, in turn, know what bad is. So you look upon different experiences or concepts and give them these labels: it is "bad" to kill someone. However, is it not "good" for that soul to be released from its earthly limitations? It's all in how you perceive these experiences.

There are many souls upon the planet who are very advanced and who are not even aware of their advancement, for they do not, perhaps, live in a publicly spiritual way. However, they are living their lives with great meaning and love and compassion for all things. There are also souls who think of themselves as spiritually advanced and yet are still living their lives in a very adolescent manner. You are all headed in the same direction, having come and gone from the Earth experience many times, learning something new and teaching something new every time, growing and developing into enlightened souls. And so, perhaps heading towards this direction is what we can call "good," and continuing the karmic cycle — not learning but instead repeating the same mistakes — perhaps we can label that as "bad." However, this is only appropriate for ourselves; it is not our place to put these judgments on others, for they truly are just having different experiences.

Greetings. It is I, Adam, your dear friend from Pleiades coming to you today. I welcome you with great love and understanding. May I answer any questions?

Hi Adam. I would like to know whether past lives truly exist?

45

Past lives and future lives do indeed happen. They are, however, perhaps not so much past, present or future, but happening all at the same time. I know this is very hard to perceive from the earthly limitation, but they do indeed exist. You have hundreds of lives upon your planet, as well as on others.

I'm trying to understand the individual consciousness that we know ourselves to have or be. When we have a memory of a past life, did we really live that past life or are we simply accessing another part of our species' consciousness, another part of our identification with every other human being? I'm questioning whether *everyone* was Abraham Lincoln to some extent or if only one soul can claim to have lived that life.

Most of the souls on your planet have had past lives on your planet. All souls have had some sort of past life. Souls do not generally share a body in any lifetime. However, there have been cases where one soul has started out in a body and left mid-experience while another soul has taken on the other part of the experience. But, I would not say that all humans have had the Abraham Lincoln experience and so on with the other beings of your planet. Each soul chooses the experiences most appropriate for them in each lifetime to live out concepts in experience form, as well as to properly play out the karmic law. Does that make sense?

Yes, that's the most common understanding of reincarnation and karma. I'm grappling with individual consciousness. I know myself to be much more knowledgeable and expansive as a soul. And yet when I'm trapped inside a physical body I have certain limitations; my consciousness appears to be confined. I guess I'm questioning whether the more expansive consciousness of my nature is linked with the more expansive consciousness of everyone else.

Indeed it is. There is the individual you that has these past lives, and there's the higher you, the higher consciousness that is indeed connected with *All That Is* — every soul, every concept, every idea. That is the part of you that is connected with God, and in that sense then, yes, you have shared these past lives with everyone. But I would not think of it in that manner. I would think of the single soul consciousness of yourself as experiencing these past lives and the higher consciousness of *All That Is* as just being. There is no past, present or future for it. Those ideas don't exist within its reality, for it is a constant. It is not limited by this notion of time.

How did Jesus become such a master on the planet at such an early time in our civilization?

Jesus came into the world aware of his spiritual self. He realized that time did not exist in the form you experience it. He came to your third dimension from a much higher place. Some souls live through the Earth experience several times and move on. Some souls never have the Earth experience. Others simply incarnate onto your Earth for the sole purpose of helping Earth beings with their limitations. When Jesus came he was sent from the seventh dimension, and as a child he had quite some difficulty with the limitations of your planet, for coming from a dimension with absolutely no limitations it can be difficult to understand basic human nature. However, as Jesus developed and awoke during his time on the planet he became aware of his connection to the Father-God, and to his spirit and higher Self, and remembered his purpose to help and teach humanity. You, too, have that understanding within you, as does everyone. Learning your purpose and making it known can help the development of humankind.

Can a soul have an Earth life and eventually die, then be reborn on Venus or Saturn, leave that planet and be reborn again on the Earth? Can this soul then leave that Earth life and choose to be reborn on another planet in another dimension in a completely different part of the universe? How does that work?

Oh yes, indeed this can work, for I have had several Earth experiences and am now enjoying my 122nd incarnation as a Pleiadian. You can choose where you want to reincarnate before you go there. Earth is going through so many changes at this time and can use so much assistance — and there are so many opportunities that are purely human — that many beings choose to continue, or come back to, the Earth experience. Others move on or decide to try a different way, much like your favorite dish at a restaurant. You know you like it and you often keep getting it. After seven times or so, maybe it's time to try something different.

Does karma compel people to make certain choices? For example, when people create certain karma on the Earth are they then obligated to forgo a vacation on Pleiades, for example, and instead required to return to the Earth to clean up their karma?

No, we also experience karma. It is a universal law that will manifest itself no matter where you reincarnate yourself. There comes a point, however, when you step outside the karmic ring and are on a path of pure service and enlightenment.

But karma does determine some of the choices that we must make, right?

Yes and no. You will always have free will, however karma will manifest itself in some way or another, as it should.

Since few people on the Earth seem to be enlightened right now and we're looking to create a more evolved civilization, can you share with us a little bit what it's like on Pleiades, what your civilization is like?

Yes. We are more aware of our spiritual existence and so we truly try to live the Golden Rule. We do not have crime or murder or rape or any of those concepts. We try to love and uplift all the other beings that are around us. However, we realize the connection we have with everything in the universe and so we also try to uplift Earth beings, for those negative vibrations do affect our planet. And while we try our best to turn them around, we would not like to see them in any form for anyone.

We have free will on our planet, but not in the same sense as you do. We have families, but not monogamy for we have many different partners, each with love and understanding. Envy and jealousy are concepts that do not exist with us. We procreate like you do and start teaching our children from an early age these concepts of love, compassion, and under-standing. We do not have school systems in the sense that you do, but we do teach our children the things we find important, which are not math and science and reading, but how to show compassion, be creative, and go towards the goals that they find important. We teach through example and play. And we take all souls who come onto our planet as our own responsibility. We don't let any go to the wayside, always listening to what they have to teach us as well.

Do you have resources on your planet? Do Pleiadians share the resources? What is a more equitable distribution of wealth, because we seem to have a lot of greed here on the Earth?

We find our ideal trade; thus, we do not have monetary distribution. Each Pleiadian does what he or she is best at and enjoys doing and they share it with the other Pleiadians. You would call this a form of communism on your planet; however, it works differently on our planet, for we make sure that all Pleiadians have shelter and food and care. We do not have Pleiadians that do not do their part. Everyone has something to share, even if it's just hugs or storytelling. We all have something beautiful to share with one another. We have learned to tap into the energy sources that are emitted from our planet and all things in the universe, including the energy that is emitted from each Pleiadian. This helps the development of our planet go smoothly.

Is it possible for you or some other being of Light to take Damiana on an astral journey with her third eye to Pleiades during one of our later sessions so that she can visit your planet?

Absolutely. I would love to share my world with her.

This has been a wonderful session. We really do appreciate your presence and the knowledge that you share. We feel very honored to have these conversations with you. Thank you very much for spending time with us.

Thank you. I do appreciate you letting me come through like this. It's a great honor on our part as well. I bid you good eve. In love and light. I shall see you again.

Being non-attached does not mean just stepping aside and watching something happen, for that's an attachment to non-attachment. It's important to find the fine line between assisting others and letting them work out their own karmic law.

9

Good afternoon. It is I, Adam. I bid you good day. This idea that human beings have of Heaven and Hell is a vague understanding of the gloriousness that awaits you after death, that if you truly live your life in service you will continue working towards this so-called Heaven and its higher expression of love and compassion. However, if you keep making unsavory choices and continue down the karmic road, you'll come back to another life of limitations, for this so-called Hell is only on your planet and is only executed from these Earthly domain experiences through war and greed and hate, for those concepts are not found throughout the universe. Thus, there is no physical place where you will go if you do not learn your karmic rule and learn from your karmic past; you will just continue on the same cycle until you learn to rise above it and move on to much more beautiful and better sanctuaries.

May I answer your questions today?

Yes, thank you. I see how this concept of Heaven and Hell relates to our last session on good and evil. How did these concepts of Heaven and Hell get started?

They were created from Earth beings who knew that you have to try and get out this cycle. They are ideas that can help influence — mostly through fear — this concept of always doing good or you'll "burn in Hell." But the truth is that you'll really just continue on the same cycle. These ideas were first conceived at the very dawn of human civilization. Although the souls who first set foot upon your planet were very forgetful of where they came from, they still had a vague sense, and so these ideas were passed down from generation to generation as guidelines, hopefully to guide humanity towards making more righteous choices.

Heaven and Hell are associated with the Bible and Christian religious beliefs. Are you saying that these concepts of Heaven and Hell were perpetuated as guidelines, perhaps similar to the Ten Commandments which were also given to humanity as guidelines?

Yes, indeed, as a vague understanding of perhaps why you should always take a higher path. While they are written about in the Bible, they were ideas passed through time before then.

But Heaven doesn't really exist and Hell doesn't really exist, not as these physical places where people eventually go after making good or bad choices during their life on Earth?

Yes and no. We create our own reality, so in that way they do exist if you believe in them. However, the idea of a fiery pit of doom where you will spend eternity, no, that does not exist in our understanding. Continuing at the limitations of Earth because you have not figured out the karmic law of understanding — that can seem quite hellish to a soul who's ready to get free. And moving on to enlightenment is quite heavenly.

What about somebody who does something really horrific on the Earth? What if they rape, torture, or kill many people and are aware that this is wrong yet they continue to do that? People like Hitler have done very destructive things to humanity that caused a lot of pain. Is this not evil? Is this not bad? Can you speak about that?

It is indeed not good. However, souls like Hitler have had their karmic law and have actually moved on. Hitler is no longer having the Earth experience. He was not punished by anyone on our side of the veil, for we do not judge like that. And while it's completely horrific and terrifying for those experiences to occur on the Earth plane, they help create compassion and move along many souls towards realizing who they want to be by what they don't want to be. And while this is a great deal of your history where there was much violence, we are hoping that humanity is past that phase and is moving on towards more global and universal love and understanding. All souls have had these immature, we'll say, experiences. You have, and I have, killed in past lives. We have learned from that and will never repeat it.

Do you have emotions like we do? Do Pleiadians and other extra-terrestrials experience feelings the way that humans do?

Some extraterrestrials do, but many do not. We are very close to humans in the gene pool and, yes, we experience all emotions very strongly, especially love and compassion. Not so much the negative ones, as we realize these are lower forms of vibration and they will not do anything to help our planet. And while we are aware of those emotions, we try our very best to avoid them. We experience humor and laughter as well.

I have some questions from our last session. You said that each soul chooses life experiences most appropriate for them in each lifetime "to live out concepts in experience form." What do you mean by that?

As a soul, you are all-knowing in concept. However, it's the *experiences* that souls crave. They must therefore incarnate in some sort of form to live through these experiences, for just having an idea and not actually experiencing it is a vague idea. For example, knowing what music is and listening to Beethoven's 9th Symphony are two very different things, so all souls crave that experience. Before you come to the Earth you create a map, a guideline, and karma will play into that. Free will — once you get to the planet — makes it so that you don't necessarily have to stick to the guideline, but you will most likely stay in that direction unless completely thrown off the path. Experiencing these different concepts that you have a vague idea about through human form — or in my case through extraterrestrial form — allows souls to understand and learn from these ideas in more complete ways.

I have some questions about karma. You said that each soul chooses life experiences most appropriate for them in each lifetime "to properly play out the karmic law." How does karmic law operate?

Whatever you put out, you shall get back. This happens with everything — every single idea, concept and thought that you put out will come back. It is a universal law. And so, in one lifetime you may put out feelings of anger, hatred or war. Although they might play out in that lifetime, often you will experience what you put out in the next lifetime.

Karma does not always play out in exactly the same way, for there are times when you have enslaved someone, perhaps. It does not mean that you will play out as a slave, although it could happen that way. Perhaps you will have claustrophobia of some sort and be stuck in an elevator, or always looked down upon for some reason that seems totally out of the box for you. You don't understand why there are these judgments against you, but they are just the karmic law playing itself out. So it goes for love and understanding; if you continue with love and compassion and service, you will rise above the karmic law for a life of service, and move ahead out of that karmic ring.

How does the karmic law actually operate? Are guides making this happen, manipulating circumstances and situations so that karmic balance occurs? Or does this happen in some automatic, mechanical way?

It's an automatic, universal law. It's infinite and it continues throughout the universe. At the very beginning of time, at the dawn of everything, karma began. Karma is overruled by dharma, however, and will eventually end when all souls realize its influence and are enlightened from it, but it is automatic. The wheels are already in motion and your destiny, so to speak, will happen no matter what.

According to the choices that we've made in the past?

Indeed.

How do we know when we are facing our own karma? Also, how do we rise above our karma and step outside of the karmic ring that you described?

Karma is happening all the time. Every situation is karmic. Noticing and learning from these occurrences will help you step out of that ring, for you must always grow and learn from these situations. Choosing a life of true love, compassion and service will move you out of this karmic ring.

Are you referring to the Law of Dharma, living our purpose?

Yes, exactly.

What is a constant? You said that certain ideas don't exist within the higher conscious reality of *All That Is* because it is a "constant." What do you mean by saying that something is a "constant"?

This is very difficult for human beings to understand, for your idea of time is linear. Yet, time is not truly linear; it is just happening, just being. There are several things that are just being. They don't exist in any past or present form. They are just existing — as is God, your higher Self, time, love, and karma. They are all constants. They are not going anywhere. They are not coming from anywhere. They just are. They will not leave; they just exist. They always will be.

Is this similar to an ultimate truth?

Yes, truths are also constants.

You said that Jesus came from the seventh dimension. What does that mean? How many dimensions are there?

There are 13 known dimensions. However, this does not mean there are not more infinite dimensions. Out of the 13 known dimensions, seven of them are of service and moving forward. After the seventh dimension, it's a place of enlightenment where ascended masters and truly enlightened soul work takes place. The seventh dimension where Jesus existed before he chose to incarnate on your planet is a dimension of service; it is connected with your dimension as well as many others. We are all moving forward. Dimensions are just forms of vibration, so Jesus was just existing at a different form of vibration — not better, just different. Many of the higher dimensions do not have the limitations that Earth has. Thus, we have achieved a more universal understanding.

You said there are seven dimensions of service. Does that include the Earth?

It does include the Earth. Whether you are aware of it or not, you are working towards service and enlightenment. All beings on your planet are working towards that, although many have forgotten.

You mentioned that Pleiadians are not monogamous. What are the advantages of non-monogamy and why do humans prefer monogamy?

We find love and compassion in all beings. We find it very restrictive to commit our love to only one other being. We think humans would benefit from this way of life, for there is so much "cheating" and secrecy that occurs on your planet. While you pretend to be monogamous creatures, you truly are not; you have several different partners throughout a lifetime — and often at the same time. However, until you raise your vibration to exclude jealousy and envy, I do not think our form of relationships would benefit you on the planet Earth right now.

Ponna from Pleiades visited and communicated with us the other day. Are you familiar with Ponna?

Yes, indeed I am.

Will she be returning or can I ask you a couple of follow-up questions on topics that she brought up when she was here?

I am sure she will return, but I am more than happy to answer any questions for you.

Ponna mentioned that the Pleiadians have encircled the Earth in a beautiful, protective golden ring. Can you discuss this?

There is a shield protecting Earth from not-so-holy extra-terrestrials. It is also protecting Earth beings from concepts that you're not ready to understand. We have taken it upon ourselves to protect you in so many ways, one of them being this beautiful golden ring.

I have a question about attachment versus non-attachment. I understand that it's beneficial for humans to be non-attached to certain ideas, to create equilibrium in our daily living. Yet, we want to have compassion for the plight of individuals. How do we balance that, and is it not true that you, as a Pleiadian, are attached to helping us humans?

Your idea of attachment is a little off, for you mean to not attach yourself *to any idea, concept, or material things.* However, it is important for you to have compassion and understanding for all other beings. Being non-attached does not mean just stepping aside and watching something happen, for that's an attachment to non-attachment. It's important to find the fine line between assisting others and letting them work out their own karmic law. We see so much potential for the human beings and we realize our connection to *All That Is*. Therefore, it is in our best interest to assist the human beings, as it is in your best interest to help others as well.

Ponna talked about trace minerals. Why did the Pleiadians coat the Earth with trace minerals thousands of years ago?

Like I said, there are many ways that we help the humans. And while at this time we cannot connect the two worlds, we do our best to help in many, many ways. These minerals are one of the ways that we help humanity, secretly and silently, for they give off energy that helps awaken many beings so they can figure out their dharma, increase their understanding, and move on towards bigger and greater things.

Ponna said that the trace minerals are just starting to take effect. If the Earth was coated with these minerals thousands of years ago, why are they just starting to take effect? What does that mean?

We put an alarm clock on them, so to speak, for we knew that at one point your dimension's vibrations would need to change. These minerals are now being activated to do their job of awakening many beings. Their energy is mixing with the energy of the planet helping to assist your movement towards the fourth dimension.

Did you know that we would need their influence at precisely this point in humanity's development? Were the minerals timed to take effect when they would be most appropriate for us?

Yes. We felt the energy of ancient civilizations on your planet and we determined that this would be the time, as the energy was headed in that direction.

Do they each have a unique purpose? Can you describe the different functions of each trace mineral?

These minerals exist upon your planet to mix with your vibrations. All of them have that specific purpose. They do not need to be ingested or even seen. We let you know about them as a reminder that we are in many ways assisting your planet's movement toward better things.

Without more details about these trace minerals and how they operate, a lot of humans would equate this with something akin to fairy dust — magic dust that does anything that you want it to do. Do you understand how humans would think like this without more details?

Yes, and I do think fairy dust is actually quite an accurate way to describe these minerals. However, they don't exist to do anything you want them to do. They are doing exactly what they should, which is mixing their energy with the Earth's energy and raising universal, global vibrations. That is their sole purpose and sole point.

Ponna said that the Pleiadians created the trace minerals by pure thought. Can you elaborate on that?

All beings have the power to create with pure thought. Many beings who have come to your planet have shown examples of this, like Jesus. Your thoughts are extremely powerful; every idea and concept that you put out exists on its own. With true faith in yourself and in these concepts, and by realizing that we are all children of God, we are all connected to God, you too can create (manifest) anything that you'd like, with the right intentions, out of pure thought.

That's a very important topic. Perhaps we can discuss it in more detail in another session. I have a couple more questions about *truth* versus *reality*. This might be related to constants as well. Ponna said that *truth* is an absolute in contrast to *realities* that we create. How do we learn to distinguish between them?

Truths are these constants; they're always going to be there. Reality isn't really real. I know that's very hard to understand, but your world and the ideas that you've created around you exist because you believe them to. Truth exists whether you believe it or not. Truth exists beyond your world, in all worlds.

What are some of the great truths?

Truths are all around you. God is a truth. Love is a truth. Karma is a truth. Dharma is a truth. Each soul's connection to *All That Is*, is a truth.

Where did truths come from? Who created them?

Truths are a constant; they have always existed. I suppose that in your understanding we could say that God created them.

Thank you for visiting with us. Once again, it was a great honor to communicate with you. Do you have anything else you'd like to share before we end today's session?

Thank you. I do appreciate these sessions. We really benefit from these connections. We love to know that our message is getting heard and understood, so thank you. I'll see you again. In love and light, good day.

Disease is a human concept. While humans can become susceptible to disease, germs are not the cause. Dis-ease in your thoughts and ideas will manifest in sickness.

10

Good afternoon my space siblings. How are you this fine evening?

We're doing well, thank you.

I did enjoy taking Damiana back to my home planet and showing her some of our life and activities (aside from talking to humanity through open vessels like Damiana, of course). I take it you'd like to do a follow-up session and have some questions about the journey.

Yes, thank you. It was a wonderful experience that was soul-stirring and emotional for us. We couldn't stop thinking about it all week. [Damiana's many out-of-body experiences traveling with her third eye, including her visit to Pleiades and her follow-up session with Adam, can be read about in *Third Eye Awakening*. Visit Damiana's website for more information: www.SummonTheLight.com]
Before I ask today's questions, I would like to set up the video recorder to document these early sessions.

Are we all set up for my big debut?

(Laughs) Yes, you are. I have a few questions about our relationship to extraterrestrials. How did humans start out on the Earth? Were we created through evolution or from extraterrestrial genetic material?

You were created through a mixture. All beings — including us, the extraterrestrials — started out as pure Light and will return to pure Light. You then manifested in many different forms starting out as vegetation, bacterial life form, animal life form, and then humanoid life form. At the very beginning of human's life on the Earth during early civilizations, such as Atlantis, humans and extraterrestrials worked side-by-side on your planet as well as on ours and others. There was some intergalactic breeding, however not entirely. We have been part of your world since this time. We have gone through dimensional shifts like you are now. At one point, we were very similar to the humans in concepts and ideas; we were not always as civilized and enlightened as we are now. However, we now find grand compassion for the humans — as you might when rooting for the underdog, seeing beings in different situations than you are in and wanting to help them. We do this with your planet as well as others.

Are you talking about Darwinian evolution, the idea that we came from the primordial pond and oceans? Did humans really originate from plants, animals and different ape stages?

Yes and no. There have been many evolutions — both of the physical body and of the spirit. Humans have gone through this Darwinian idea. However, spirit has experienced life as vegetation, as microorganisms, as animals, and as humans. You will continue on to extraterrestrial and back to Light. These types of evolution are happening at the same time.

How did the human DNA code evolve or was it created?

It did evolve in the Darwinian manner that you speak of, from organism onward. However, DNA is only a manifestation of the physical body in which Light, or spirit, has chosen to physicalize itself. And so through universal manifestation and development, DNA was created, as was *All That Is*.

Is humanoid genetic material stored somewhere or is it easily available to higher beings of Light through this manifestation process?

This DNA has developed through time and is now accessible to all souls wishing to manifest in physical form. It started out, however, through pure manifestation.

Is DNA ever modified by extraterrestrials or higher dimensional beings? Is anything added to or subtracted from the human genetic code to create adaptations to physical bodies on the Earth or to develop completely new physical bodies on different planets?

The Grays are working with their DNA code as well as the human DNA code to do just that, for they no longer can breed in a natural manner. They have to clone themselves, so they are vigorously working to create a false DNA code through subtracting from humans and themselves. On the planet Earth there has been some delving into this, although we don't suggest that your scientists continue.

Did this occur during Atlantean times? Did the Atlanteans experiment with the genetic code by mixing DNA?

They did experiment with DNA, and this was, among other things, part of their destruction, for it was unnatural at that time — and now — for these codes to be mixed. It will create a new form that cannot be naturally produced.

Can human physical bodies be altered to vibrate at a higher expression or will this only occur when we become more enlightened by our own efforts to improve our thoughts and actions?

Your vibrations can be raised naturally. This is the most sophisticated and technological manner. It is accomplished through loving one another, through compassion, through enlightenment, and no other way.

If we all started as Light and will eventually end up as Light, what is the purpose of physical existence.

To have these experiences. Light is pure being, pure love, pure God, but to experience the many different physical opportunities that there are, we take on these different physical expressions. And so we feel what it's like to be a plant, and for many eons we experience that. And then so on with organisms, animals, and humans.

I usually think of reincarnation as the idea of souls reborn into new human bodies. You're describing spirit actually entering into and ensouling plants, bacteria, and animals. Is that correct?

Yes, over time, however. This is not occurring in your understanding of present time, for it's the *evolution* of spirit, while reincarnation is the *karmic expression* of spirit.

What is the Pleiadian history? How many civilizations have you had?

We too have experienced many civilizations and lives. Many of us have had experiences on your planet lifetimes ago. We also reincarnate and have very similar DNA to humans, for we can be described as a future, advanced humanoid civilization.

Did you say earlier that you have been working with humanity since Atlantean times or has it been longer than that? If we have similar genetic material, there must be some kind of ancestral link between humans and the Pleiadians.

We are your future. We are linked and have been working with the humans before Atlantean times, but we worked with the humans *physically* during Atlantean times.

Do Pleiadians have what could be described as a karmic relationship with humanity?

Not in the sense that you're thinking. We have compassion for humanity. We see it making choices that we've made in the past and we'd like to guide you towards a better future — like an older sibling assisting a younger one who's making the same choices that we made.

How did you get to where you are today? During your early history did you have similar problems like we have on Earth today?

Yes and no. We on Pleiades have developed over time from experiences on Earth and other planets. This incarnation of Pleiadian beings has reached a place of higher dimensional enlightenment; we are trying to assist others in the same way.

What does it mean for you to describe yourself as a Pleiadian? Here on the Earth we can see the star cluster of Pleiades, but these stars are hundreds of light years apart. What does it mean to be from Pleiades?

We have many sister planets and incarnate on one of these planets. Just like you call yourselves the Earthlings, we call ourselves the Pleiadians. It would be similar if you were to call yourself the Milky Ways, although that sounds a little silly at this time, doesn't it? It's just a label that you on Earth can call us to understand these enlightened beings from the seventh dimension, who wish to assist your kind.

Are you actually located in the physical region that we understand as the star cluster of Pleiades?

Our planets are, but we travel all over the universe. Yes, that is the location of our planets in our dimension.

I have several other questions. Would you like me to ask them now or would you prefer that we wait for a future session?

While I am eager and excited to answer them, I think that perhaps you should save them for tomorrow or the next day. Is that all right with you?

Absolutely.

All right. I wish you a wonderful evening with love, light, and high vibrations. I bid you good eve.

We are not here to preach our ways, to start a new religion, to convert anyone, or change anyone's preexisting ideas. We are here to help move along and assist those who ask for it as you move into a higher dimension.

11

Good afternoon. It is I, Naor. How are you on this fine day?

Hi Naor, welcome. We are doing well, thank you.

May I offer some insight into your questions today?

Yes, how would you and other extraterrestrials like to help humanity? What is it that you can offer us?

At this time we would like to continue coming to you in this manner, offering our guidance and know-how from experience. We would like to assist humanity towards enlightenment — becoming more civilized, cultured, and understanding, as well as compassionate and loving towards all beings of the universe. We would like to help human beings become more aware of their spiritual existence and assist in the raising of their vibrations into higher dimensions. Once we feel that the energy is at a safe vibrational level, perhaps we can meet face-to-face to assist humanity in controlling the depletion of the atmosphere and making your planet safe for future generations to continue inhabiting.

If you were permitted to directly communicate with higher-ups on the Earth, what ideas and concerns would you convey?

Extraterrestrials do communicate with higher-ups. Unfortunately, not all of our ideas are being heard. If I were to talk to some of the higher-ups — which, I might add, is not something I would like to do because I prefer talking to open vessels who understand and accept what I'm conveying, like yourselves — but if I were to speak to them, and they were open, I would convey how important it is that you start paying attention to your environment, for it is being destroyed. The values that many of the beings on your planet hold are so backwards to what is truly important in the universe. The businesses and multibillion dollar companies that are destroying your planet — through physical destruction as well as corruption and greed — are not important. That is only perpetuating those beings' karmic cycle on your planet. It is so important to find love in your heart and compassion for all beings — especially other beings on your planet — for so many are pushed aside and not taken care of. Just listening to and assisting other beings will help change vibrations and ideas on your planet.

What is the difference between your group of extraterrestrials from a planet that you call LaZarus, and the Pleiadians who we have been working with as well. How do you differ from the Pleiadians?

We are more extraterrestrial in your visual idea of form. We do work with the Pleiadians although they are in a higher dimension than us at this time. However, we are all working towards a higher goal of enlightenment. My group, as well as the Pleiadians and other extraterrestrial groups, are all assisting on spiritual enlightenment through physical form. Thus, we are trying to assist our little brother, planet Earth, as well.

Do you actually live on a physical planet that you call home that is located somewhere out in the physical universe?

We do indeed. However, until your vibrations are raised into a higher dimensional plane, we will be invisible for the human eye to see.

Do you have specific intervention plans to help humanity grow and create a more civilized culture?

At this time we are feeling out humanity's energy. As much of your planet awakens and is heading towards the fourth dimension, we feel there will be a time when we can assist your planet safely — for our safety and yours. Our plan to intervene at *this* time shall be through our conversations, guidance, and word-of-mouth. At a future date, perhaps we will arrive safely and share with your planet different ways of life, if the people will let us.

Are you able to protect us from ourselves and guide us to stop acting in unenlightened, dysfunctional and self-destructive ways?

Unfortunately, no, we are not able to protect you from yourself; you are indeed your greatest enemy. We can only offer our hand in guidance, show through conversation and example a more enlightened way of living, and hope that you will not let your ego get involved. Realize that we are only here to help. We do not judge; we just wish for you a better way of life. Our offer is always on the table, but we will not interfere with free will and we will not assist if we are not directly asked to help.

If in the future more of humanity requests your aid, will you arrive in the physical or continue working with us mainly through channeling? And if you do come, how long do you anticipate staying with us?

For now, it will be solely through channeling. At some point we do hope to meet in physical form (and the way your energy is headed, we do see that occurring). If we do meet, we hope to assist your planet so you will not destroy yourself and we can continue an intergalactic relationship for many, many years to come.

What are some of your most serious concerns regarding humanity? Are there any immediate threats to our continued existence?

Like I said, you are your greatest danger. It is imperative that you find alternative energy sources and tap into the magnetic fields that are within your planet and the energy fields that are within each of you, for your atmosphere is being depleted. Many diseases that exist, and more to come, are negative immediate results from depletion of your atmosphere and your environment. Nature helps to keep you in balance and alive but you are destroying it. The corruption, greed, and ego of so many beings on your planet are continuing their karmic existence. It is imperative that they find love, compassion, and equilibrium in their hearts, discover their karmic purpose, and assist the many souls on your planet who are barely surviving the wars that are still being fought over religion and land. You must find a mutual way of life.

What are some of the things you appreciate most about humans? What do humans need to learn?

We look upon human existence with love and compassion. We see a troubled child that we can assist and guide towards a more enlightened future. We are encouraged and excited by beings, such as yourselves, who accept us and are conscious of what they are doing in their life. We do see love and compassion on your planet, so much potential for growth, and encouraging signs that change is possible. The ego, greed, corruption, and anger — these low forms of vibration — sadden our existence, but we do not see humanity as a lost cause and we are eager to assist you.

Please speak about global warming.

Global warming is a direct threat to humanity. Although many of the animals on your planet will learn to adapt, it is sad that some will not. The depletion of your atmosphere is creating a critical relationship to your Sun which is, in turn, affecting your atmosphere, weather, and earthly elements. The hurricanes, volcanoes, earthquakes, and fires are all directly related. There is a cause and effect relationship. Besides becoming aware of it and taking more care of your environment, we don't see humanity correcting this without extraterrestrial assistance.

Do you actually have technology to dissipate or transform CO_2 and other pollution in our atmosphere?

There are advanced extraterrestrials, like the Pleiadians, who do have spiritual manifestation technology within themselves to assist you.

Our world economy seems to be teetering and tottering. We nearly had an economic collapse a few years ago and we're not completely recovered from that. Please speak about economic stability.

Yes. This is all a direct result from the complete and utter imbalance in your economic classes, for it is not natural to have a very small amount of your population controlling all the wealth while the greatest percentage of your population lives without food and shelter and with disease. Until there is a balance economically, where these select few learn to live without — realizing that true happiness is not from economic hierarchy but occurs through love, compassion, and shared understanding of ideas and spirituality — there will be this imbalance. We do not see your economy redeveloping in the near future, for we see a rise in power from those who do not share values that are truly important on your planet. And so, the way we see energy now, it will be quite some time before it balances itself out.

Please speak about the potential for peace between Israel and Palestine.

We do not see this resolving itself without some sort of white flag being raised from either side. Right now, both are like two rams butting heads and it would take one of them to lay down for the fighting to stop. Peace will not be realized until concepts and values are raised, when true understanding and love for each other — and for themselves — are reached.

Please speak about food that is made with genetically modified organisms (GMOs). Is it safe and something that will feed more people on the planet or is it dangerous and a threat to natural food?

Genetically modified foods are not natural. They are causing unnatural effects on hormones in humans. We would like to see more focus on, and production of, naturally grown produce and food to feed many people, for you do not need to alter food; just focus on making more of it naturally. However, the destroying of your planet in so many ways has created a need for these altered foods.

Some GMOs are designed to protect food against pests that would otherwise destroy crops. Growing food organically can be problematic due to pests. What are the alternatives?

There are natural "pesticides" — other animals and insects that can help protect these crops. The chemicals and pesticides that you are using now are very dangerous to human existence. By spending more time with the natural way of life, instead of killing these bugs — which is killing the food chain for other animal beings on your planet, as well as hurting the humans — you can continue the natural chain of food.

Did GMO technology come from humans or was this given to us by negative extraterrestrials?

Genetically modified food is mostly from human development. However, some extraterrestrials have also delved into this category. Other extraterrestrials on other planets are having the same results and issues. However, they did not share it with the humans; it was fully manmade.

Do some extraterrestrials intentionally provide bad information to humans to hurt our civilization?

There are some extraterrestrials who, like humans, are not aware of their spiritual existence and are not working towards enlightenment. Some of them are dark or evil, greedy and mischievous. So, yes, there are some, but you need not worry about contact with them.

Did you say that some of them are evil?

In your concept of what is valuable they are part of the dark side, so to speak, just like there are humans that are part of the dark side.

Please speak about terrorism and its impact on the Earth. What are some possible solutions for us to deal with it?

Terrorism, which is linked with karma, is an unfortunate part of your world at this time. While those souls involved in it are on their karmic path, it is important to continue living your life in the most uplifting manner possible as shown by example. There will be dark moments on your planet, but we see the energy as a whole heading towards a better existence, although you are not there yet.

What are we as a civilization doing to create or contribute to these beings who seek to cause pain, death and destruction through terrorism?

You are just being. Much of your civilization has gone astray and their values are slightly backwards. So some beings, instead of showing compassion and trying to help your civilization, would rather destroy it, for *they see* the values as being off. However, their values are just as backwards. They observe these values in your civilization because they are projecting them.

Please speak about technology, its role and impact on our civilization.

We see that your civilization has advanced quite rapidly over the last several years. You've made quite some leaps and bounds technologically. However, we feel that you are focusing too much on technology and not enough on what is natural and spiritual and truly important in your world.

Would extraterrestrial help be considered interfering with our free will or would not helping us eventually cause the Earth to become uninhabitable for humans and animals?

Not helping would eventually do that and we offer our assistance. It is your free will to take it or not. We are not going to come down in a couple of years and magically clean up your atmosphere and make your world a beautiful, natural place unless you seek out and ask for our assistance.

A retired captain in the Air Force and former missile launch officer provided evidence that a UFO was seen hovering over U.S. nuclear missile silos shortly before the missiles malfunctioned and could not be launched. Do you know anything about this and could you speak about whether or not that would qualify as some sort of an extraterrestrial intervention?

We are slowly making our presence known and we do offer our assistance when those situations arise. There are times when some extraterrestrials, like the Pleiadians, intervene without you asking, for it's like a little child who you give free rein about the house, but the child keeps running towards the fire. You eventually put out the fire.

Please speak about the role of parents and education towards a peaceful world.

Right now we see quite a lot of dysfunction within the role of the parent — not taking responsibility for their actions and not leading by example. We would like to see parents more involved in their children's lives, taking more time out of their so-called busy days to teach and play with their children, to instill more real, valuable rules and guidelines for a better future.

We might have to teach our parents how to teach and play with their children because many of them seem to be trapped in a cycle of dysfunction from the way in which they were raised.

Indeed, and it would take a global change of more involvement and less of the values that are put into your children today about money and what they should be looking for in life. We would also like to see a different educational system for your children, for they learn in so many different ways and this standardized idea of learning does not suit every soul.

That is a very important topic that perhaps we can discuss in greater depth another time. Thank you for visiting with us. Do you have anything else you'd like to share before we end today's session?

I do appreciate you taking the time to let me speak on what we find important. I wish you a wonderful rest of the day. In love and light, I bid you good day.

12

Greetings. It is I, Adam. How are you on this fine day?

We're doing great. Thank you, Adam.

Excellent. I shall start off our conversation today discussing communication on your planet, for so much of it is lost in context and meaning. Fifty percent of communication that is often forgotten is listening. So many beings on your planet forget to listen and are more wrapped up in being heard. They also cover up and hide so much of their meaning in deception and negativity. On our planet we speak telepathically. This may seem strange, for so many beings on your planet feel like that would be invasive. But when you have no negativity and you wish no ill intent upon anyone and you're not ashamed of your thoughts, telepathy really is the ideal way of communication, for nothing is lost. Intent and feeling are immediately understood by the being receiving the information. One day, perhaps, you too shall receive this point in your communication.

All beings are creators. Every single moment of every single day you are creating and manifesting your reality. It has become so second nature to you that it goes completely unnoticed, but every day, everything you see, everything around you, you created. You are part of the Source. You are part of God and you, too, can create anything you want in your life with proper intent and manifestation. May I answer any questions today?

You introduced two different topics. One is on communication and the other is about our own creative nature that manifests everything in our world. Let's start with telepathic communication and empathy. In an earlier session, Naor said that they are very similar or even identical. He implied that Damiana is using empathy through her telepathic processes. Please discuss this.

Yes, they are indeed two in the same, for with telepathy not only are you communicating and understanding meaning, you are actually taking on the feeling and intent of the person who is sending the information. No meaning is lost in this form of communication, making it entirely ideal, for in normal speech so much is lost in intent. Take for example a sentence such as, "I hope you are having a wonderful day." In a plain sentence, the full meaning is unknown. And with the technological aspect that humanity has now instated, even slight intent and different nuances in the messages are completely lost. With empathy, the entire meaning and context are fully understood.

Are you saying, for example, that with internet email people lose context, that we don't know whether they are being sincere or sarcastic?

Absolutely. So much is lost with your current form of communication, for so much is said without saying.

What do Pleiadians think about sarcasm, when people are sarcastic because they think it might be funny?

We enjoy humor, and sarcasm can be a silly way to relate to each other, but when it has ill intent, as it often does on your planet, we don't find the humor in it. However, when it is light-hearted and relatable between two beings, we think it is a fine way to find mutual compatibility.

What other ways, besides listening, would you recommend for humans to improve our ability to communicate with each other?

Listening truly is key, for almost everyone wants to be heard. So truly listening, setting aside your ego and your drive to be heard, truly, truly listening, hearing what others are actually saying, would solve so many problems on your planet.

Are there any other communicational techniques that we can learn to improve our relationships with others?

Truly listening and relating to each other, understanding where each person is coming from. When a person starts to get defensive on a topic, instead of fighting to have your view heard and then creating an argument, step aside, take a moment to consider why they're getting so worked up over this topic. Why are they so passionate about it? Are they afraid? Are they worried? Understanding where they're coming from and relating — even if you do not agree — but understanding and relating, truly create a more ideal playing ground for communication.

Please talk about the other topic that you brought up, how we are constantly creating our realities every day, perhaps even in automatic or unconscious ways.

Absolutely. Every minute of every day is created, for reality, as we've discussed before, isn't really real. It is, to say the least, a figment of your imagination and you instantly create this reality around yourself. There is a mutual agreement and understanding that you have with other beings that it is real, but it is all manifested from pure thought by each and every one of you. You can manifest so much more in your life. Whatever you want in your life you can have, you can create, because you have done so before.

What about this couch that Damiana is laying on. Did I manifest that? It seems like somebody actually built it out of real, physical material. How would that tie into this conversation?

It is real because you and other souls on your planet have agreed it is real. It is a mutual agreement that everything physical around you — physically created on your planet — is real. There are also concepts and ideas that you cannot see that are just as real. Is love not real? Is air not real? Everything is only real because you've made it real in this physical form on this physical plane. In other planes you also create your reality, but you are more conscious of it, for you are more all-knowing and not in an experiential state of mind.

You gave two intangible concepts of reality: love and air. However, I thought that love is a constant. I'm not sure if air is a constant because it's made up of molecules. Can you clarify this?

Indeed. I was just giving examples of concepts of reality on the physical plane that are agreed upon by other beings and yourself. The love that I was speaking about is love on the physical plane, not the constant, all-powerful Love that runs within *All That Is* — more of physical love on the physical plane. I should have clarified, I apologize. Love is indeed a constant like truth, God, karma, and dharma. Air is made up of so many molecules and is a flow of creation from the relation between you and your environment. It does not exist throughout the universe, but only within certain planets.

When I knock on wood, it feels very solid and real. Is everybody on the Earth just under some sort of mass delusion when we all agree that a chair is solid and real?

It's real because you agree it's real. I wouldn't call it a delusion, per se, unless you want to call this whole physical reality a delusion — which we could — but it is real in your reality.

How does consciousness relate to physical reality, physical matter? Do rocks have consciousness? What about atoms, molecules, and quarks; do they have consciousness?

Not in the sense that you and I have, but they do have life, a spark. They are different. It is not consciousness, but they do have their own life form.

So, is the spirit of a being or a thing separate from the consciousness of the being or the thing?

In some cases they go hand-in-hand, but in an atom or molecule or rock it's more of a spark that is created. This is the problem some of your scientists are having, for they are able to create that spark and create life, but not true spirit and soul; they don't understand the difference.

You seem to be saying that some living things, like humans, have a physical body and a soul. However, even though scientists might be able to clone another body, they can't create the soul.

Indeed. A soul could enter into a cloned life form if it chose to but most souls would not choose that experience.

Is it also true that a soul would choose not to enter into an animal, plant, or mineral form because it would be too confining?

Yes. However, we have as souls over time gone through phases of plant form and animal form and now the human form for yourself (and extraterrestrial for myself). We experienced life as plants with those limitations for those experiences, and so on with animal and human, as we will then move on to different forms with less limitations. This is happening in a linear time frame as it appears to you, and it is happening simultaneously in the great Now as well. And so, there are beings inhabiting mineral, plant, and animal forms, experiencing that, and then they will move on to different forms in the future.

How likely is it for a soul to be born into a human body with human experiences in one life, and then incarnate into a more highly evolved extraterrestrial existence, such as Pleiadian, in the next life? Can human spirits incarnate into Pleiadian bodies or are other planetary systems more ideal for certain souls?

For certain experiences to karmically take place, certain choices and planets are more ideal. When you rise above the karmic ring and are on a path of true service, there comes a point where choosing a Pleiadian life, or other dimensional lives, becomes more ideal.

Would you and other Pleiadians welcome the soul of Hitler onto your planet or would it be more ideal for his soul to go somewhere else?

We would welcome any soul on our planet. We are without judgment of his time and experiences on Earth — and he has reincarnated and lived another life on Earth. He is now living in the astral plane and is quite aware; he will not live the life he lived again. We will welcome him — or any other souls who have learned from their mistakes — open-armed on our planet.

If a soul has karma to balance, would that keep it from incarnating on Pleiades?

There are certain planets that are more ideal to work out karmic law. Pleiades is not one of those planets at this time. Although we are affected by your karma, we are in a higher dimension and living a life of pure service towards humanity and other planets in the universe. Souls not incarnated are aware of this, therefore a soul who still has karma to work out would not choose to incarnate on our planet.

Are there any Pleiadians on the Earth today who were born into human bodies?

There are many Pleiadian souls on the Earth helping in disguise as humans.

Does this make them more likely than the average person to manifest positive energy and humanitarian instincts?

Indeed. They are solely on your planet to help guide and serve humanity. That is their only intention on your planet.

Do they also have to contend with the possibility of forgetting their true purpose here and getting caught up in the karma of the Earth?

Absolutely. They are, however, more likely to stick to their path. But they of course are living the human life and can easily get wrapped up in what is human.

Do they run the risk of having their lives regress into more karmic problems that they will then have to clean up in future lives on the Earth?

If they stray that far off the path, then they could get caught back up in the karmic ring. However, I don't see them straying that far.

Do you have access to the akashic records? How expansive is your capability when sharing information with us?

We are incarnated like you are, and while we are more advanced at this time and further down the path of enlightenment, we, too, are not constantly all-knowing. But we are in touch with our spiritual side and we can access akashic records through meditation like you can. We also have so much more experience and understanding at this time than you do which helps us guide you along.

If we invited people to join us during these sessions and they asked personal questions about themselves like who they were in a past life, is that something that you would be willing or even able to answer?

We would probably be able to help with that, yes.

What is the average life span of a Pleiadian?

We live between 100 and 200 of your Earth years.

The Bible describes people living more than 900 years.

Human bodies actually have the capability to continue living. However, over time the soul has realized that it can achieve more by reincarnating into a fresh, new, young body — the newest model, so to speak. So instead of continuing in this body with wear and tear, the soul has set a time limit that is more ideal to reincarnate.

Is it more ideal for Pleiadians to live 100 to 200 years and then give up their bodies to reincarnate into newer ones?

Indeed.

You said that you are incarnated. Do you have a physical body of a higher vibration?

It's a physical body of a Pleiadian. We are in the seventh dimension, so our vibration is different than yours at this time.

Is the body that you occupy different from ours even though you have similar DNA to the humans? Is it a more refined body of Light?

It's a physical body vibrating on seventh-dimensional vibrations. When you rise into higher dimensions — for example when you move into the fourth dimension — you will not lose sight of the third, second and first dimensions. Your vibrations, while higher, can still operate on these lower dimensions, so you gain and do not lose.

I have some questions on another topic. Do germs cause disease?

Yes and no, for disease is a human concept. And while humans can become susceptible to disease, germs are not the cause of disease. A lowered immune system through emotions and thoughts can make you susceptible to the many viruses and diseases that are on your planet.

How does a virus cause problems? Is it because we have dysfunctional thoughts and ideas?

That is a large part of the problem. Your lowered immune system lets in these viruses which then mutate in your body creating illness and disease. But dis-ease in your thoughts and ideas will manifest in sickness.

What is the best way to protect against epidemics of disease?

The best way to protect yourself is living your life in the most wholesome and spiritual way, living with only positive energy, for this negative energy can lower your immune system. Taking care of your temple, your body, in the most beneficial way will also build up a wall so that all defenses are holding up against disease.

What is an ideal way to protect babies from contagious and potentially dangerous diseases?

Babies normally enter your world in the most wholesome and healthy manner. Unfortunately, your doctors have actually created a way to damage their natural immune systems. Their perfect, little bodies are immediately being injected with disease, which then mutates and causes harm.

Are you talking about vaccinations that these babies receive?

Indeed, for they are not necessary. Your babies have been born in a perfect state for hundreds of thousands of years.

What about epidemic diseases? Many young babies have died from measles and polio.

During those times when babies got such diseases it was either from neglect or a choice the soul made upon coming into life for karmic or experiential reasons. Today, the diseases that are placed upon babies are not necessarily a choice of the soul.

Parents aren't always neglectful. They might love their baby and yet sometimes it is exposed to a disease and dies. Is it always due to karma? There must be an alternative to protect babies.

Cures for many of the diseases on your planet are available. There are natural remedies throughout nature in plants and herbs on your planet to help assist in these diseases.

What is an ideal diet for most humans?

Different diets are ideal for different humans, but sticking to natural, organic, non-genetically modified or hormone-infused foods would be better for all humans. Producing more of your own food and eating less from the large manufacturers would be better as well, for they often do not have nutrition in your best interest.

Is it okay for some humans to eat meat?

Some humans do better from a meat diet. However, the way in which much of your meat is being produced is not appropriate or even beneficial to the health of humans.

Do you have anything else you'd like to share with us today?

Thank you so much for letting me come through. Have a wonderful day. I will return soon. Love and light.

Peace on your planet is coexistence without harm to one another; this is achievable. Each of you can reach this place of inner peace within.

13

Greetings, space siblings. I am Ilana, a space sister from Pleiades. We are so eager and excited to see the many sacred Indigos blooming all across the world as we speak, for so many starseeds have awakened. The alarm has gone off and the transformation is taking place. The starseeds' purpose is to create change within the masses, question authorities in charge at this time, and set pace for a new beginning. For too long, human beings have continued in the footsteps of their predecessors, not questioning where they are headed or proper morality. It's time for constant questioning of all ways of life, stepping outside the given path, drawing outside the lines. Going along with certain ways of life simply because you were told to, or because that's just the way it's been, is no longer an acceptable way to be. It's time to redefine humanity, blurring the lines between the physical and spiritual divinity within everyone, shedding the scaly skin of times long ago and breathing in the fresh, new air of the Golden Age.

Can I shed some light on your questions this evening?

Greetings, Ilana. It's nice to have you with us today. You mentioned morality. Please elaborate on that. Are there any absolute morals?

Morality is to be defined by each individual, realizing these morals for yourself, not because society or culture or civilization has defined what is moral, but being guided with love in your heart, with intuition in your mind, and realizing what is truly good. Discovering what is proper for your spiritual growth and the spiritual growth of all of humanity is essential when considering these morals. Universally, love for *All That Is*, is an absolute. Coming to this understanding through your own discovery is most important.

You also discussed *authority* this evening and put forth the idea that we should question authority. Since our society is run by authorities and appears to be dysfunctional, perhaps we need to look elsewhere for our guidance. Some people look toward spiritual guides for answers. Do you have any suggestions? If we're going to question or turn away from our current authorities, where else should we turn for higher guidance?

Question everything you hear. Question it within yourself, for you and only you can know what is correct. Your society at this time is constantly looking outside of itself for answers and guidance, while all you need to know is within. Taking time to go within each and every day will truly open doors and windows that have been shut for eons. It is imperative that the beings of your planet come to this understanding and stop looking to so-called experts and authority figures for what can be answered within their own hearts. Living in the dark — not doing the necessary research or coming to these conclusions on your own — can have the utmost saddening effect upon your personal being and your planet.

How do we establish a more ideal or utopian civilization? What are the principles that should guide a civilized society?

Take time to listen to and follow your own intuitions, making sure that all decisions are coming from a place of higher love and compassion. Set the ego and individual needs aside. Look for a more universal and civilized answer to your questions. Act more globally, helping *all* beings on your planet. Properly raise your children with love and compassion, teaching them what's truly important in life. Setting aside what your society currently thinks is important can set the pace for a dignified and ideal civilization.

What is an ideal form of government?

That is something your society will have to come to terms with. However, it seems that the present government is not meeting all the needs of the people at this time, so we would look to a more global self-governing nation where more people are heard and more people can make decisions for themselves through proper research.

In the United States, which is a very powerful country on our planet, we have a capitalistic system driven by competitive urges to improve our products and increase monetary gain. Is this a good system or does it have too many flaws to meet the needs of a global society?

Do you need me to answer that for you? Is your economy where you would like it to be at this time? I think it's time for the people of the United States to look within and discover what best meets the needs of the people, and perhaps it's time for a change.

Many people in the United States argue that it's not fair to redistribute wealth, that people with the most money earned it and shouldn't have to share it with people who have less. What do you think?

Those beings are on their karmic path and it is not for me to place judgment. However, we do hope and we do see a future where there is more universal understanding for your brother and your sister, for you are all from the same Light and you are all made of flesh in physical form. We hope those beings reach this understanding, for we wish to see your planet reach a place of global and universal enlightenment — not leaving these beings with more egotistical views behind, but raising them to a better understanding.

What is an ideal educational system? How should we be educating our children?

Again, that is something the humans will have to agree upon. But we do see a time to totally mix up and change the way things have been done for so long. We would like to see the children of Earth learn through more experiential means, with more time and development placed on proper, universal care and education for the children, teaching values of love, compassion, and understanding — showing them the beauty of the planet, with less time wasted in classrooms on tests.

Do you see the world going into a darker place before we begin to move into greater Light? Do you see the probabilities leading toward more economic and financial distress worldwide in the next few years? Do you see a shakeup of our economic system?

Yes. However, sometimes the most growth can arise from the darkest of nights — like the Phoenix rising out of the ashes.

What do you recommend to people with higher awareness and open hearts? How should they live and prepare for the future?

They can focus on who they are and what's important in each of their lives. They can spread love and joy in each interaction every day, and while being aware of these dark times, not letting it affect their vibrations. They can spread love and light through change, for these are the beings who will lead your planet to the new dawn.

Adam said that most souls would not choose to incarnate into a cloned life form. Why would souls be less inclined to be born into physical bodies that were cloned?

Certain aspects are lost without the natural reproduction of humanity. It's important for many souls, for karmic purposes, that they don't lose these aspects in their reincarnation.

Why is it more ideal for a soul to reincarnate into a new, younger body rather than living in the same one for many years? Continually having to start over again as a baby relearning many things doesn't seem efficient.

Reincarnation is for karmic purposes, as well as turning in the old, weakened body for a fresh one with new experiences and new concepts to learn upon the planet. It's important to experience births in different countries as well. Instead of constantly going to Disneyland for vacation, it is like reincarnating and experiencing Sea World. You would get old and lose karmic understanding in the same life.

If a soul experiences karma as a result of past negative actions but does not perceive or understand the connection between the cause and effect — and perhaps even thinks that it might just be having a run of bad luck — does it really learn a lesson?

Maybe, maybe not. There are situations where the soul is not aware that they are cleaning their karmic slate, but they are, for they do not want to repeat the same mistakes they made in the past. There are other situations where they do not learn and they continue on this karmic cycle.

If the idea of karma is to learn from our mistakes, why is it possible to sometimes experience it in ways that are not clearly connected to our previous infractions of karmic law? How can karma truly be balanced if a previous infraction of the law is not recognized?

It is recognized, you just don't realize that it's connected to this previous karmic past. There are experiences where you have learned and have grown; you just don't realize it. For instance, perhaps you have lots of love and understanding for animals in this lifetime, but in a previous lifetime you were cruel and did not find worth in animals. In this lifetime you are not remembering this previous past life, but perhaps in your child-hood you were exposed to animals in a way or manner that made you fall in love with them and see them in a different light. You had no prior knowledge of this past life, but you are learning and growing from it.

Thank you for that explanation. Aurora said that the *Law of Karma* operates on several different levels. What did she mean by this?

She meant that karma operates throughout lives, within lives, and throughout the universe. It can be a small karmic debt to be paid or a large karmic debt, and it can be changed through understanding.

Please talk a little bit more about the *Law of Dharma*. Is this the law that means everyone has a spiritual purpose?

Yes. Dharma is above karma. Finding that purpose and dedicating yourself to a life of service and purpose and helping humanity will raise you above the karmic law setting you on a path of dharma towards enlightenment.

How can people find their dharmic purpose?

For many beings, it seems like a path of trial and error. However, when you are on the right path for you, it will be one that you are truly passionate about. You are doing it because it is what you love doing. It is what you feel is best to grow spiritually and help humanity — not because of monetary or idealistic reasons.

Please speak more about the *Law of Within*: whatever is within us will be manifested outside of us.

If you hold on to anger, hatred or envy towards another person, you will in turn create conflict which is then inflicted upon yourself. By spreading love, compassion and understanding, love, compassion and understanding will be returned to you.

How does that law actually operate? How is it possible that what we think and feel inside of ourselves is somehow projected onto the world around us and then experienced by us?

It is a universal constant. Its manifestation works throughout the universe in everything you put out. Every idea and concept — everything that you say, make, do, and think — is projected into the universe and then reversed in a mirror image which is then sent back upon you. It operates all on its own throughout everything that is.

What occurs between lives? Do souls plan out their future lives?

Some souls do. Some exist in between lives, experiencing and guiding. Some reincarnate in other life forms upon the astral plane and the higher planes.

Speaking of the higher planes, Adam said that there are 13 known dimensions and that humans are on the third dimension, moving toward the fourth; Pleiadians are on the seventh dimension. Can you discuss some of the differences between the dimensions?

These dimensions exist around you all the time. There are different levels of enlightenment in each of these dimensions. The first through seventh are dimensions of service and growth. The eighth through thirteenth are dimensions of teaching and guidance.

Do future lives really exist in the present or are they just projections of probability?

Time, as you are aware of it, would create these future lives. However, time exists as a constant — not linear, but circular — creating these past, present, and future lives all occurring at the exact same moment. This is very difficult for humans to understand. However, as you project into the fourth dimension, time will be more easily grasped.

Is it possible that humans are a projection of higher consciousness — our own higher Self — and that, like the images on a movie, if we were able to look at the entire film strip we would see the beginning or ending frames and could pick out any moment in time, so to speak, but that only when it's being projected onto a screen does it appear as though each moment follows previous moments?

That is a very intuitive way to look at it and, yes, that's similar to how it works. While it's laid flat, it would seem linear, but it is actually happening constantly all at the same time. Your higher Self is connected with *All That Is* and your lower self, living this life, is only conscious of what is going on right now in this third-dimensional life.

It's still a very difficult concept to believe that my future lives have already taken place, especially when it seems like they're based upon probabilities existing in the present moment. Seth, who spoke through Jane Roberts, talked about *probable selves* where all probabilities exist in some other parallel universe. Is there anything to this?

Parallel universes are an entirely different subject. They do indeed exist, and choices that you make have several different outcomes. There are parallel, infinite amounts of *you* existing within these different parallel universes.

Why do we have so much hatred and war here on the planet Earth?

There are polarities upon your planet for karmic reasons and to help teach many souls a life of compassion by viewing or experiencing a life that they do not want to lead or live again. It's learning what they want to be by what they do not want to be. As you move into a Golden Age, we see a future for humanity with hatred and war being a thing of the past.

Why do we have polarities on Earth? Is it not possible to know love without hate?

No, not *true* love, unfortunately, so polarities and basic, most instinctual relativity teach you true love through true hate.

I have a question on dark matter. Scientists believe that conventional, physical matter only accounts for about five percent of all matter in the universe. They posit the existence of dark matter and dark energy. Do these exist, and if they do are they related to planets in other dimensions?

Dark matter does exist. In this infinite universe that is continually expanding, continual dimensions are being created, and until they are viewed in vibrational form they will constitute as dark matter.

Do these other dimensions have something that is similar to matter on the third-dimensional plane?

Some do, some do not. Some have concepts and ideas that are too advanced — beyond the human brain's capacity at this time. Until you move into these higher, vibrational dimensions, it's too difficult to even comprehend.

Can scientists measure higher dimensional vibrations or qualities with our instruments here on the Earth?

Not at this time, but perhaps you'll be able to at some point.

Adam said that Pleiadians communicate telepathically. Do Pleiadians also communicate through the use of voice language?

Rarely. We have found it much more efficient and more direct to communicate telepathically and through empathy. This avoids language barriers or misunderstanding.

Under what circumstances would you communicate through voice language?

When interacting with beings who have not reached a state of telepathy.

Are the Pleiadians responsible for any of the sacred texts on the Earth? Were these provided by extraterrestrials?

There are texts like the Dead Sea Scrolls that have been influenced by extraterrestrial beings (not the Pleiadians). We did interact upon your planet during Atlantean times helping and guiding, but we did not leave any sacred texts.

Have you considering doing that? It seems like a positive way to influence humanity for the better.

Perhaps, but we are not here to preach our way of life. We do not want our views and ideas to become a religion or to be worshiped or influence beings who are not ready to join our understanding of how to empower your planet. So, at this time we will not be placing any sacred texts upon your planet.

Who are you and why did *you* come through today instead of one of the other Pleiadians that we've previously worked with?

I am just one of the many ambassadors for Pleiades. I, like many Pleiadians, am eager and excited to speak through this open vessel and see how my voice is heard. I do appreciate you welcoming all of us into your life and into your home.

Thank you. We feel honored to communicate with you. Do you have anything else you'd like to share with us before we end today's session?

We are truly honored to speak through and discuss these many different topics. We are so encouraged by beings such as yourselves and the many beings that are now awakening and creating change upon your planet, for we are excited and eager for the uplifting, empowering movement that is ahead within the next several years. I bid you good eve.

Play is the physical manifestation of joy and ecstasy. It is very beneficial for humanity to continue playing into adulthood, taking time to have fun, to laugh, to enjoy each other.

14

It is most important that change occurs in each individual from within, for it will then be reflected outside among all of you. Each individual must discover their place of love and compassion for humanity, setting aside ego and greed. It is I, Ilana. May I answer any questions today?

Hi, Ilana. Yes, I have a couple of follow-up questions. Please talk about the starseeds. Who or what is a starseed?

Starseeds are technically within all human beings. However, several individuals have come to your planet to help inspire and create change at this time. The starseeds, or Indigo children, are awakening and creating the change that is needed in your society and world. They are slightly different in idea and demeanor. You can recognize them by their willingness and openness to accepting new ideas, and their compassion for other beings. They aren't afraid to try new things or step outside the box. They aren't afraid to be different.

What about Crystal children? I've heard this term used as well.

Crystal beings is a term for the newest generation of starseeds. The young babies and children of the last 15 years or so are the Crystal generation, the same way that the starseeds of the 1980s and 1990s were referred to as Indigo children. There will continue to be terms for the starseeds, but they are all just souls with love in their hearts, here to help guide and create change upon the planet.

Have all generations had their own starseeds or advanced souls dedicating their lives to service?

Indeed. Your generation has had quite a few starseeds. *Your* work and dedication have always been greatly needed upon your planet and *you* have helped create change needed within society. You were never afraid to go a different way. You weren't afraid of looking silly or different, questioning everything. This is something that is instinctual within the starseeds.

Will Indigos and starseeds provide solutions or will they just offer rebellion against the current systems?

Both. Many Indigos will shake things up, offering rebellion and change. However, many starseeds throughout the planet are also offering solutions, creating a different dynamic for the planet. The Crystal children are offering love and compassion in areas that the Indigos have shaken up. The Crystals will soften the blow.

Do people who are technically not here as starseeds have the same capacity? Can every human soul reach a deeper place in their nature, be of service, and bring about positive change on the planet?

Absolutely. Starseeds are within everyone on the planet. You are all from the same Light. However, some souls on your planet right now are still working out karma — they're stuck on the karmic ring — and are not yet at a point of awareness of their spiritual divinity, who they are as spiritual beings. They are not there yet but they will be at some point. Everyone has the potential for great things.

Earlier you said that morality is best defined by each individual. If everyone determines their own morality, won't this lead to some sort of social chaos?

That potential is there. But when looking for morality, if you do it with love in your heart and intuition in your mind, the same results should emerge. Always do *everything* with love and compassion. Everything will come together with love and compassion.

Which countries on our planet have the most enlightened types of government?

There are small tribes within Africa and Australia where they are still self-governing. Agriculture has not become globalized and everything is within the tribes. Working towards family and love, and using natural food, has worked for these tribes for hundreds of years. They do not have one person leading; all their ideas are heard. This works for the small tribes. For larger nations like the United States, we think government similar to ones in Norway and other European countries would work better. Communism in idea could also work, but not the way it's working in China. You would need some alterations before putting it into practice.

Many people in the United States are very opposed to any form of socialism, although everyone gets a monthly social security check when they become seniors and most people like driving on highways that were paid for by tax dollars. Is a socialistic system similar to communism?

A socialistic system is very similar, and while idealistically it could work, I don't think the United States is at a place to accept that right now.

Well, we're sure not going to accept communism.

Absolutely. The United States is going to a darker place before it gets better, but it will get better.

I noticed that Damiana hesitated on the last answer. That brings up another question. Is a deeper meditation required to receive more pure channeled information?

Deeper meditations are not always necessary for the most pure channel — just the most ideal frequency and that idea within her head. She will get to a better place with time. Today she is slightly off with the connection, for her health, I think, is distracting her.

How much of the purity of the information is Damiana responsible for and how much of it is in your control or the control of the beings who speak through her?

We try our best to get our message across in 100 percent of its entirety. However, until we feel that Damiana is ready, it is still being filtered through her thoughts and ideas, and some of it can be lost in translation. We *will* come through in a much more distinct form.

I've noticed with other channelers — even popular mediums — that much of the information seems very clear, very pure, yet some of it appears to have been filtered through the ego and biases of the individual bringing forth the information.

Even the best channel can have an off day and the connection can be different on different days. Sometimes the ego and the channel's own thoughts can muddy the water. We hope to keep working with Damiana, rousing her to her own third eye travels while we come through so that you can get the most pure and unfiltered messages from us.

I have a few questions about planets and dimensions. Why do some beings have their experiences on planets while other beings simply exist in other dimensions?

For karmic purposes, planets are often the most ideal place to have the many experiences that they offer. Dimensions offer different opportunities in growth and teaching. And while in soul form you can go to these many different dimensions, everything is conceptual. Living on the planets in physical form creates the experiences.

Please describe beings who exist in higher dimensions where ideas and concepts predominate.

Ascended masters, archangels, and advanced souls exist within these realms. There are concepts there beyond your comprehension, but these beings are there to help guide younger souls along who haven't yet reached that point.

Are you saying that ascended masters, archangels, and advanced souls are in these higher dimensions to help younger souls to understand more advanced concepts?

They guide younger souls on their journey where they are now. And they, too, will one day reach these higher planes.

Do the beings who live in these higher planes have a social network and interact as a unified civilization?

Do they interact as One, is that what you're asking?

I suppose that I can only perceive it from my limited perspective. Here on the Earth we have different cultures that make up a planetary civilization. The Pleiadians live on their sister planets interacting with each other within a distinct civilization as well. I'm asking if the beings who exist on these higher planes — in these dimensions of ideas and concepts — also operate within this idea of a civilization.

No, not so much. They exist beyond that. They are unified as One, connected to the higher Source, as are all of our higher Selves, but they do not exist in your idea of a civilization.

Do they gather in a particular region of space or is their domain without boundaries?

Their domain is without boundaries.

Well, thank you. Do you have anything else that you'd like to share with us before we end today's session?

I do appreciate you letting me come through. I will be back. Thank you again. I bid you good day.

You manifest by being — changing your vibration to match up with the vibration you wish to create — for wanting only creates wanting, the longing effect, while being creates just that, what you are trying to create. So, being that change will create that change.

15

Change will happen, so going along with it and going with the flow is in your best interest. Universal laws exist: You are One with *All That Is*; What is within, goes without; You do exist in any type of form — and that form will continue changing as it always has and always shall. Change is one of the constants. Being aware of change yet not letting it affect your vibration is most important.

Creating the life you want is quite attainable. Visualize it, speak of it and be it, for when you project yourself in the direction that you want, you open up your vibrations to match up with the vibrations of that which you would like your life to be. Taking time each day to set these goals will help move your life in the direction you would like.

When you place judgment on a person or a situation, you are immediately creating that judgment within yourself. When you say that a person is mean, you are immediately creating that meanness within yourself. So it is important to be discerning but neutral in situations, always raising up the vibration, never lowering it.

It is I, Naor. May I answer any questions?

Hi Naor. Why aren't these principles taught on the Earth? How come more people don't know about these very important principles, like this idea that when we judge others we're judging ourselves?

These are ideas and concepts we would like to see taught in your school systems. We think they would benefit the children of Earth, helping them to grow into more wholesome, loving human beings. Unfortunately, at this time these little gems of truth are to be sought out by those who do not just look at the surface, but dig under it to find the true treasures. We hope to see these concepts taught one day.

I have some questions about children, so it's pertinent that you brought this up. How should children be honored and taught?

Children should be welcomed into the world. This is extremely important, for they truly are your future. They should be raised with love and understanding, spending time with them and, while setting boundaries, letting them explore what excites them, letting them discover the many beautiful things on your planet for themselves. Children should be given choices and treated with respect and honor, as you would like to be treated. Many of the children coming to your planet today are old souls who have the utmost potential if brought up properly, and with your assistance can extract their potential to help your planet.

Do you think parents should be required to take a course on parenting before they can have children?

We cannot insist on something like that, however we would like to see more awareness brought to the parents before choosing to give birth, more balance in the adult's life so they can properly give the attention and love that the children need.

Should the world community be allowed to stop certain cultures from teaching children harmful concepts? For example, should we disallow the perpetuation of hatred toward different groups of people?

We would love to see that come to an end but we can't lecture our ways on other people. However, teaching children harmful ways of life should not be allowed. Humanity will have to come to some sort of unity on how you're going to put an end to this, for it is one of the challenges that you will have to face to bring enlightenment to the masses.

Do parents on other planets raise their own children, or in advanced cultures are children cared for by the larger community?

On many planets it's the care of the community. We consider our children to be children of the planet; parents care for their children as well as all children. We have found this to be beneficial in raising and sharing the love of the children. So the children, while still getting the love and care from their parents, can safely go out into the world and experience the same love and care from all the grownups of their planet. Some planets are still raising children like it is done on Earth; we think there are benefits to both ways.

I have some questions about relationships. How do people find happiness in their relationships?

By being true to who they are, finding trust and honesty in their relationship, and not trying to change themselves or their partner. By creating a balance in their relationship, they will find happiness.

How do they attract those relationships?

Put it out to the universe, as with anything you would like to attract into your life. Visualize it, vocalize it, and live it, and you will attract that into your life.

A lot of people ask about soul mates and twin flames. What is a soul mate and is it different from a twin flame?

Soul mates and twin flames are generally the same thing and there can be more than one. Soul mates are created from past, present, and future lives; they are souls that have made agreements to reconnect at another point in time. And, like I said, you don't have just one of them; there can be many. This is a concept that humanity has not yet realized. They think there is only one true love for each being, but there are many relationships that you can experience with many different souls throughout many lifetimes.

Some people believe that twin flames are different from soul mates, that they were originally a single being that was split into male and female halves when it left the Creative Source. Is this true?

You are all connected — higher Selves are all connected. Two souls can agree to incarnate into separate bodies. In that sense, it is a split. However, in that sense we are all twin flames.

Why do some people prefer homosexual relationships? Are gay relationships less natural than heterosexual relationships?

They are not less natural at this point in your culture. A soul can make many choices for a map of their life. So, many souls make a connection with past lives, with the same sex perhaps, or they're just going to have a different experience stepping outside the norm of your society. Thus, when they incarnate, they often have karmic or other experiences that can create the basis of heading in that direction. But it is usually thought out and prepared beforehand by the soul.

Are you saying that souls choose to become homosexual for specific purposes or experiences that they desire on the planet?

Yes, exactly.

Why is homosexuality forbidden in the Bible?

Because at the time when the Bible was created it was, throughout humanity, a time of procreation, and it was very important, the spreading of the seed. Homosexuality did not allow that at the time. However, homosexuality has existed throughout history, even during Bible times, although not as prevalent and open as it is at this time.

Why are so many people uncomfortable with homosexuality?

Because of concepts of sexuality that your society has inflicted upon you. You have been raised to think that homosexuality is inappropriate. With time and new generations these ideas will change, as did ideas about interracial marriage.

Why are humans such sexual beings?

It's one of the many experiences that souls keep returning to Earth for, and to procreate so more souls can have the Earth experience, and because sexuality is one of the few energies that humanity has tapped into. There are many energies around you that you can tap into and use in the future, but right now sexual energy is one of the few that you know of.

What does it mean to tap into sexual energy? How do we use that energy other than for sexual procreation or pleasure?

You can harness all the energy around you, including sexual, for spirituality or more advanced concepts. This is the idea behind the Kama Sutra, although that is still a very basic use of the energy.

Are you saying that Tantric sex has spiritual benefits?

Yes. Using that sexual energy and merging it with the spiritual energy can create doorways for spiritual awakening.

Is it truly a sexual energy or is it simply biological or biochemical changes in our body?

It is both. Physically it is biological, but it is energy that becomes sexual in nature.

Is our society oversexed?

In some ways, yes. Your sexual nature has gotten out of control and your society has become too focused on this sexual energy. They could benefit from toning it down and discovering other energies upon your planet.

Or transforming the sexual energy into different expressions?

Yes, that as well.

Are there any sex acts that are shameful?

We don't find any sexual act shameful. We do not judge personal preference.

What is the spiritual reason for sexually transmitted diseases?

There are many diseases upon your planet and the spread of them, sexual or not, is part of karmic purpose — there are karmic reasons for them. Also, natural cures have been found, but in humanity's infancy they are not being used and this must be properly addressed.

Speaking of natural remedies, please discuss the healing properties of plants.

Plants all over the Earth have medicinal and healing properties. Your scientists are aware of many of them and make some of them available but keep others hidden. Many of the plants are used in western medicine and many are used in eastern medicine as well.

Are options to heal ourselves being suppressed? Is the medical and pharmaceutical industry too controlling over our health choices?

They are much too controlling over your health, for there are benefits and cures from these plants that they keep hidden. They distribute what they feel will maintain control of the population. This is not appropriate for your planet.

We should be permitted to take herbs if we believe they could benefit us, yet our regulatory agencies have the responsibility of deciding whether we need to be protected against ourselves. They don't want us to be fooled into taking herbs with unproven benefits when drugs are available.

You should be able to take these herbs, for they are on your planet to help you.

Is marijuana a gift to humanity from the plant world or should it be avoided?

Marijuana has several benefits for humanity and it helps many people in pain going through illnesses. It is a gift to humanity, as are many plants on your planet.

What about using marijuana for other purposes besides alleviating pain? Some people use it for recreation. Other people use marijuana to expand their mind and think in different ways.

We don't see marijuana as a problem on your planet. We think people should be able to use it for recreational purposes. However, *depending* on it or on any other substance for full awareness and mind-opening experiences should be limited, for true spiritual awakening is found within.

What are your thoughts about using hallucinogenic mushrooms, LSD, or Ayahuasca to stimulate spiritual experiences?

All have their benefits on your planet and should not be limited. You should be able to experience these different mind-altering substances in a most appropriate way for yourself. However, for true awakenings, going within is most ideal for your benefit.

Thank you for coming through today, Naor. We always appreciate your visits and insights. Do you have anything else you'd like share with us before we end today's session?

Thank *you*. I always appreciate these exchanges as well. I'll see you again soon. I bid you good day.

You do not need to use fear in your life. It is a low vibration; you can raise yourself above it. There is nothing to be afraid of. You exist in every form and will continue when you are no longer human.

16

I'll start off today's discussion talking about religion. What is religion and why are there so many different ones on your planet? Religion has existed in some form or another since Light first manifested in physical form upon your planet. It was that connection to a higher source that Light still remembered, but it had been become veiled through the transformation. So several advanced beings reincarnated on the Earth and left small records throughout your planet to remind humans that they are all demigods. Their words rang true as they spoke to so many people, but through time many of these words became warped and lost meaning.

All religions started from the same spark and the same idea. However, like anything in the universe, change must happen. And so, religion must change through diversity. Having these many different religions gives options on your planet for choices and ideas, and each reality has some truth. It is important, as with any idea or concept, to 1) discover these ideas on your own, not going along with what the others around you or your ancestors have been doing, but what you truly feel in your heart is most appropriate for your reality, and 2) as with any idea, question it; do not put all your eggs in one basket, so to speak. The many beings on your planet were never meant to be empowered by putting all their faith in a single being or a single idea. Discovering their truths on their own, and how they are connected to the higher power, is most important.

It is I, Naor. May I answer your questions today?

Good morning, Naor. Thank you for coming through. It's interesting that you started today's session on religion because I prepared several questions about Jesus and Christianity. Who was Jesus?

Jesus, like you and me and all beings on your planet, started from the Infinite Love Source. He came to your planet from the seventh dimension. He came with a mission to spread love and remind many beings of your planet who they are and where they came from. He had the same power that every being has. However, he had no doubt and no lack of faith in this power that he possessed and the power of his connection to *All That Is*. So he went on his mission spreading love and joy and healing many people. Many of his ideas have been misconstrued and are way off course. There have been many others who have come to your planet with this same mission.

What was Jesus' early life like?

Jesus came to your planet as all souls do. When he entered this world, he started out confused, not sure how to harness the power that he knew he had inside. When he was a child, there were many incidents where this power was not used in a most appropriate way. At times, he seemed wild and out of control, and he spoke of concepts, even then, that were beyond many of the humble village people of the time. All who came into contact with him realized that he was different, that there was something special, even though they could not quite grasp it or understand what it was. However, with time he grew up, realized how he could help many people of the planet, and remembered why he came.

Did Jesus come from a virgin birth?

Jesus came from a pure and sacred birth, as do all Earth beings.

Is that all you wish to answer on that question?

Virgin in your culture holds an idea of pure innocence, and in many cultures this idea of virgin is held above as sort of a pure concept. In that sense, Jesus came from a virgin birth.

What was it like to experience the teachings and healings of Jesus? What did people feel when they were in his presence?

The many miracles enacted by Jesus, and energy he exuded, was pure love at its highest potential. Feeling this love through him empowered many people. It was also confusing and emotional, for they didn't understand all of it at the time, but they felt many emotions they had never felt before. You too — all beings — have this potential to feel that pure love, where you are part of that and your vibrations can match that.

Are you saying that everyone on the planet, by feeling love within their nature and by wishing to share that love with others, can also heal people and create miracles in other peoples' lives?

Yes, every single one of you has that potential. You are all of the God Source. You are all of Love. Everyone has the potential to manifest, to heal, to create — you are all creators.

What happened when Jesus died? Did he plan on being crucified?

Jesus was all-aware of his future with the crucifixion. When the Roman guards came to take Jesus, they felt his love, they felt his energy. So they did not take Jesus; they took a doppelganger that Jesus had put a protection on. It was indeed his secret twin who was crucified instead. But he felt no pain, only love as he hung on the cross.

That's a phenomenal revelation. I have never heard anything like that before. What was Jesus' intended reason for being crucified or for having his twin crucified?

He was aware of the anger and conflict that his love and healing was having on certain people. So he knew he would only have a certain amount of time on the planet. He was aware that over time his death would create a new understanding on the planet.

Is Damiana's connection okay today or does she need to take a moment to reconnect?

We are well connected. She is a little in awe of some of the discoveries we are speaking of today and she is making sure she's hearing everything correctly. Please continue.

Do you perceive that Jesus' purpose for being is well represented on the planet? Have humans internalized the principles Jesus taught?

Unfortunately, we think many of his teachings have gotten lost in modern society. Many of his ideas have been turned around and misconstrued. Basic ideas and concepts are still taught thoroughly to the masses, but not necessarily always followed. With time, hopefully people will not take the text so seriously and realize it was a very simple message of pure love. It's very simple: Love will conquer all.

Is Christianity as it is practiced today a good example of what Jesus would have wanted? Are Christians generally more spiritual or closer to God than people who follow other religions or belief systems?

Individuals are close to God and *everyone* is part of the God Source. Christianity in some ways has warped many of the ideas and concepts that Jesus taught — and which are, unfortunately, not necessarily practiced. Jesus, much like Buddha, never intended to create a religion. He hoped people would find their own power, their own sense of the Creator, and spread love through their own discoveries and understanding. This has become widely misconstrued throughout your world.

Many people believe that to be a good Christian you have to convince other people to accept Jesus into their hearts and convert people over to Christianity. Do you have any comments on this?

That was never the intention or teaching that Jesus had or hoped for. He is, as we are, completely nonjudgmental, and hopes all beings through their own discovery identify who they are as demigods — physical and spiritual beings. Preaching and forcing your ways on someone else was never part of Jesus' teachings.

Is there any significance regarding why Jesus happened to be Jewish and ended up being the centerpiece of a Christian belief system?

There's no real significance other than change, and as I started off the conversation, religion must change. How it changes, however, is up to the masses. You, too, can influence future transformation of spirituality.

Did Jesus choose to be Jewish because many of the Jewish people of the time had religious views that needed change or that could have used an infusion of new ways of understanding?

Yes. Many of the practices back then were very harsh and it was time for change and time for love to spread. Many of those ideas got lost and misconstrued.

Does the belief in extraterrestrial existence conflict with what Jesus represents?

Not at all. Jesus, while on Earth, was very aware of extra-terrestrial life and has always been open to *all* ideas. Of course, now we too have a connection with Jesus and his love.

When an extraterrestrial such as yourself speaks through someone's mind, like you're doing with Damiana, is its value immediately discounted from a biblical Christian perspective? In other words, are Christians likely to reject these conversations simply because the Bible seems to warn people away from associating with otherworldly spirits?

Many people on your planet view the world and then alter it to fit around their belief systems. This has been done with the Bible. There are many accounts in the Bible — if not the entire Bible — of people speaking to God, speaking to angels, (and even references to extraterrestrials). Many people have considered it different from channeling. It is not, for channeling is as old as the beginning of time.

Is the information that extraterrestrials provide by speaking through Damiana mostly for starseeds and light workers or is this information also meant for Christians and other people on the planet?

It is meant for those who seek it out. We are not here to preach our ways, to start a new religion, to convert anyone, or change anyone's preexisting ideas. We are here to help move along and assist those who ask for it as you move into a higher dimension. You are our space brothers and space sisters; we wish to help you out if you'll let us. But we will not be inflicting these ideas on anyone who disagrees. They are on their path living their life and their reality. It is not for us to choose if it's wrong or right or change it. The people who this information is best suited for will be attracted to it and they will come. The nuts and bolts and cogs of the universe are all in motion and it will happen the way it should.

Thank you for that clarification. Do we have time for more questions?

I have as much time as you require, for it does not exist for me.

Well, then maybe you have an infinite amount of time.

Or none. (Smiles)

Please elaborate on the idea that by judging other people we are really judging ourselves, or that by calling somebody mean we are creating meanness in ourselves.

Think of it in the opposite terms. How do you feel when you give someone a compliment? You can't feel upset or angry when you do that. You instantly receive the same gratification and emotion that you put out, and so it goes for these negative emotions as well. It is not nice to call someone mean and you will instantly feel that meanness. You don't always recognize it as you're projecting it out and observing it in the other person. But it is instantly reflected back upon you. This occurs with all things in the universe, as this is a constant that will always happen until you rise above it and remain neutral to different situations. If you remain neutral, this will end a karmic manifestation of these negative thoughts or ideas or words. Always staying on the positive will keep you in good light.

In an earlier session we briefly discussed sexuality. I have a few more questions. Where does sexual energy come from?

Sexual energy comes from biological (physical) energy, as well as from many other energies that are within you. Humanity is sexual-based on many levels, so this energy gets manifested in a sexual way. This energy is within you and within everything and it has the utmost potential. You have the potential to tap into this energy and use it as a resource, for it does not need to be wasted or projected through sex. It is real and can be harnessed; you can use it.

Well, I don't think that most people on the Earth are going to believe that using the energy for sexual pleasure is wasteful, but I understand what you mean. You're saying that humans have biological energy that we mainly utilize for sex although it can be used for other purposes.

Indeed, and it is just one of many energies that course throughout the body.

Where is this energy coming from? Is it coming from within the body?

This energy is part of who you are. It comes from within and can be projected outwards and spread to and from different beings. There are many energies to be harnessed. "Adrenaline rush" is another energy that has potential for humanity.

Do we have an unlimited supply of this sexual energy or adrenaline rush energy?

You can create it within yourself, so yes it is unlimited.

Please explain how sexual energy can be transmuted for other purposes, especially for spiritual use.

For spiritual purposes, you can use sexual energy — the very basic ideas that you have with your Tantra and Kama Sutra. Not releasing this energy in sexual ways, holding on to it and focusing on it gives it more power and energy. You can meditate with it and focus on it. As humans progress, these energies can be developed and used once again — as during Atlantean and Lemurian times.

That leads into my next question. Can sexual energy be converted or harnessed into useable energy on the material plane, for example as a force to move or lift objects?

Yes, I spoke about this in an earlier session. As you move into dimensions that are less dense, these ideas and concepts will be more focused upon by certain scientists of your planet and they will learn how to use this energy and harness it, for it has potential.

In an earlier session you said that we can combine the Earth's magnetic energy with the energy that exists within each of us. Were the pyramids built this way?

Yes, Egypt was one of the first civilizations existing with Atlantis, right after Lemuria. They were in a fourth dimension at the time and these energies were still readily used.

If early civilizations were in a fourth dimension and we are now in a third dimension trying to rise back up to a fourth dimension, what happened? How did we trip down to the third level?

During the history experience you know as the Great Flood, which washed out Atlantis and pushed you back under the water, it lowered the vibration on your planet, for it affected your whole planet. And Atlantis, during its end years, was using technology for inappropriate purposes that the people weren't quite ready for and this knocked down the vibration. You've been in the third dimension since then.

Perhaps we can talk more about that later. Thank you for coming through. Do you have anything else you'd like to share with us before we end today's session?

Thank you. As always, the pleasure's all mine. I bid you good day in love and light.

17

Breathe. Relax. All shall unfold as it should in due time. There is no need to force it or rush ahead, for patient beings are rewarded with true understanding and divine knowledge. Greetings, it is I, Aurora, from Alpha Centauri. May I answer any questions today?

Yes, hi Aurora. Thank you for coming through today. We haven't heard from you in awhile. Please give us a brief background reminding us of who you are and what it is that you do. With whom is your group associated, and how do they work with the Earth?

We on Alpha Centauri are part of the Intergalactic Council. We are protectors of the Earth, as well as many other extra-terrestrial groups. We are associated with the Pleiadians and are also in the seventh dimension. In addition to our role as protectors, we are also ambassadors, taking this opportunity to communicate, spreading love and light upon Earth's plane.

How does your role as an Alpha Centauri differ from the role of the Pleiadians, or of Naor from Lazarus who is also working with us?

I am just one of many who wish to speak through. We *are* different and accomplish our roles throughout the universe. Coming through with words of wisdom may not allow you to differentiate at this time, but later on the differences between us and our messages will become clear.

Is it okay to ask you the same types of questions that I would ask the other extraterrestrials?

Ask away.

Naor was with us the other day and spoke on religion; I have a couple of follow-up questions. Naor said that certain records were left on our planet and that several sources have joined our planet to remind us that we are demigods. What records were left, who were the sources that joined our planet, and what does it mean that we are demigods?

All beings, all souls, are connected to the higher Source. You are all part of God and you are your own individual sectors of God; you are all demigods. There have been several extra-terrestrial communications between your planet and the universe — from Egyptian hieroglyphs to Dead Sea scrolls to crop circles. These are all records of the different communi-cations and reminders of our time shared upon your planet in the past, reminders of times long ago when communication between extraterrestrials and people was common. When the time is appropriate, many other records will be discovered. However, their sources may remain a mystery while being given credit to ancient cultures.

Naor said that many beings came to our planet with the same mission as Jesus. Could you talk about some of these other beings?

You're quite aware of many of these beings: Mother Teresa, Gandhi, and Desmond Tutu, to name a few. Others have gone on without public notice. There are many who have come with the pure purpose of spreading love; they are among you to this day. You, too, have this point and this purpose, as all humans have this potential. You all have the potential that Jesus had; that was his main message that got lost over time.

Naor said that Jesus did not die on the cross. Instead, the guards took a doppelganger that Jesus had put a protection on. Please explain this concept and how that was done.

When the guards came to take Jesus, they instantly felt the love that surrounded and emanated off of him, and they could not continue the task. Jesus was aware that the guards had to take him or they would meet their demise. So they took instead a man who looked just like Jesus, and Jesus put a protection on him. They took *him* to the cross instead. Jesus said goodbye to his disciples and went off into the wilderness to speak with God to figure out the next best plan of action. He then returned three days later, removed the man that looked like him and let him go on living.

Where did this man come from? Did Jesus manifest him or was this just a man in the crowds that looked like Jesus?

Jesus manifested his lookalike to look like him, but he already existed on your planet.

You said that Jesus came back three days later and freed this man. Could you explain that?

Jesus put a protection on this man, so he was in a type of coma state and was pronounced dead. When Jesus returned, he released this man and continued on.

What happened to Jesus? Did he keep living on the Earth?

Jesus ascended after this incident. He came back, had a last message for his followers — a message of love and light and that they too had this power within them — and then he ascended, for he knew his time had to end on the Earth.

This information about Jesus is provocative. I'm interested in another controversial topic. Are you able to answer questions about astrology?

Indeed.

Do the planets in our solar system affect human behavior? Is there a true relationship between celestial and terrestrial events?

There is a relationship between *all* that is. *Everything* in the universe is connected, and, yes, astrology is a small percentage of these celestial connections. At your birth, when you enter into the physical plane, you are immediately connected with the planets and the universe.

Do the planets actually affect human behavior or do they simply mirror human behavior?

It's more of a mirror. They do not affect your actions. It is a cause and effect on your part, not the planets. The planets simply act as a manifestation of your connection to different feelings and experiences on your planet.

How does the time of birth link a person to the planets in the sky?

The rotation and location of the planets at the exact moment of your physical manifestation on the Earth is your connection to the physical world. It is your individual link while on the physical plane.

Is the weakness of astrology today due to its imaginary, make-believe influence or because we don't yet fully understand the laws by which it operates?

Both, in a way. You create your reality; I cannot say that enough. Everything that you have in your manifested reality on the Earth is created from you. However, there is a link between you and everything in this universe, and astrology is a tool to understand that link.

Do other solar systems in other galaxies have similar setups where sister planets bear an influence over the planet of incarnation?

Indeed, and your Earth has an influence on us on our planet in our dimension as well.

Do planets in other solar systems provide a different framework for spiritual growth and development than the one established by the planets in our solar system?

There are different archetypes that different planets can mirror. Some may be similar to Earth's. However, other beings who have different experiences on their planets, with different concepts and ideas that you aren't aware of at this time, will have these archetypes mirrored on their planet.

Do planets act like vessels for great beings in the same way that our bodies act like vessels for souls?

Indeed, and this continues infinitely throughout the ever elastic expanding universe, from a tiny speck of dust to the most enormous star; they all mirror celestial bodies.

Do these celestial bodies have beings or essence or spirit or soul inside them? For example, does Venus have a great being using the planet like a body for different purposes the way in which my soul is using my body for different purposes?

Indeed. Have you not felt your Mother Earth's energy before? All the planets have an essence within them.

Do individuals have power greater than the astrological influences? Is the soul of a person greater than the birth chart?

Yes and no. Your influence and your connection with the universe is made up instantly when you are born, but your soul, when not in physical form, goes beyond that and embodies *All That Is.*

Do early childhood experiences correlate with karmic purposes and synchronize with astrological influences?

Yes. Your time of birth and connection as you enter the Earth is all mapped out for these different karmic purposes and different influences that will happen during your time on Earth.

Are astrologers today correctly interpreting the essences of the planets or is there more to know?

There is always more to know. However, like I said, these archetypes are mirrored from your planet, so astrologers are correctly interpreting archetypes that are seen throughout the history of Earth's time.

Do planets actually *cause* events in our lives or do the events and astrological influences simply happen at the same time?

It is all connected and planned out by you beforehand. The planets are not causing this; they are simply mirroring your connection to the universe and to these different archetypes and events at this time on your planet.

Can astrology be considered a timing device for the unfolding of important growth opportunities in our life, pinpointing when certain events and karmic experiences are likely to occur?

Indeed. It's one of the tools that humanity has for understanding their purpose, their "cause and effect" on the planet, and their connection with the universe. It is overlooked by many, though.

In that regard, can astrology be considered a gift from God, a divine tool given to humanity from higher intelligence? Are there other gifts to humanity similar to astrology?

Indeed, it is a gift — and up to you to understand how to use it. There are many gifts on your planet. Life itself is a gift from God. And your creative influence in creating your future and who you are on your planet, is a gift as well.

Some people use the tarot as a spiritual tool. Others use the I Ching or numerology. Do you have anything to say about other techniques that people use trying to understand human nature or higher principles?

As I said, you are connected with *All That Is*. You are connected with numbers, symbols, art, nature, science — everything — and these connections can be identified and used. So, yes, these are all different ways to understand humanity.

Damiana has a question. Are people affected by the karma of their ancestors? For example, if your grandparent was a Nazi, would you be responsible for some of the negative energy that was created?

Some souls carry over this energy, but not all of them. And so it is up to the individual whether to release that karma or hold on to it. There is potential to hold on to the karma of an ancestor, but it is not necessary.

Would you say that people create their own karma and it is not passed on to others? Are we ever responsible for the karma of our relatives?

Sometimes you take on that karma but you do not have to; you are not responsible for it. You are only responsible for your own karma, your own actions.

Why do people experience anger? What is anger all about?

Anger is a lower vibration. It's your will against another's or something else in the universe; it's your reaction. It's not necessary. You do not need anger in your life. When an event does not go your way, or someone has a different view, you can make a conscious choice to not let it affect you negatively — to look for the good in it and to realize that it's all part of the purpose of the universe in your time on this planet, and this time will be over at some point. It's not the end-all, be-all, and your soul will continue. So, releasing that anger, making conscious choices for higher vibrations in your life of love, joy, ecstasy, and compassion, are all positive vibrations that you can exchange for anger.

Do dimensions also manifest as different colors?

Vibrations manifest as different colors, so higher, vibrational dimensions will manifest as different colors, for color in general is just different vibrations of light.

Physicists today say that the universe is expanding at an accelerated rate. Will the universe continue to expand at an accelerated rate or will it eventually boomerang back and contract into itself again?

It will eventually boomerang back. However, the universe is infinite and it'll boomerang back into infinity. You will continue as a soul — as a spark of Light — when this eventually happens. This will not affect the Light.

At the beginning of today's session you talked about being patient. Was that a personal message for us or a general message to everyone? I wonder if you want us to be more patient with Damiana's development and sharing this information, letting the process unfold naturally.

It's both. You should let this unfold as it should, but I'm not telling you to refrain from pushing the development and unfoldment along. However, forcing and pushing too hard too soon can have the reverse effect. Therefore, being patient with humanity and releasing this information when it feels right has the utmost importance.

I don't have a clear vision yet of where Damiana's channeling is leading us, and I don't fully sense or understand the differences between when you or Adam or Naor comes through. I could be speaking to the same entity, but you have all indicated that at some point in the future your personality or essence will be clearly distinct from those of the others. Is that correct?

That is correct. With patience and time, and as Damiana develops her different gifts, the differences between all of us — as well as the similarities — will become more clear.

Do you have anything else you'd like to share with us before we end today's session?

I do appreciate you letting me come through. We will continue working with you and Damiana; everything shall unfold as it should, with due time. Please be patient with the process and with us. Have a wonderful day. In love and light.

18

For the last few decades your society has been riding a wave of technology, drifting along into the future with this concept that technology will bring more ideas and profit. It's time to realize that without the basics, without a good grasp of what is truly important to humanity at a root level, it all becomes fluff without filling. It's time to realize that growth and balance are needed throughout your culture, developing from the inside out basic, seemingly simplistic concepts: love, compassion, and understanding for your brother and sister. These basic ideas are lost every day, replaced by monetary greed and corruption — silly concepts that have no true potency.

You will influence change by changing *your* concepts within yourself, always coming from love and the heart chakra, creating balance from root to crown, making sure all of who *you* are is complete. Then you will influence those around you.

May I answer some questions this evening? It is I, Adam.

Yes, hi Adam. It's very interesting that you brought up technology as one of today's topics because my first set of questions is about Atlantis. Please discuss earlier human civilizations such as Lemuria and Atlantis.

Lemuria settled before Atlantis and was quite expansive, extending all the way from your Australian-Oceanic area today through India, Africa, and all the way to your Hawaiian Islands on the other end. There were many sister islands as well. Lemuria was a spiritual-based civilization that mostly consisted of beings with celestial bodies, although they could physicalize themselves if they chose to. They were in the fourth dimension and did not have this restraint of time placed upon them. Technology, while advancing, was not one of their prime gifts. They led with love and compassion and were ever pondering their existence, as they were rather philosophical and eager to understand energy and magic. Over time, sister or daughter civilizations developed from Lemuria. Atlantis, rooting from Lemuria, developed and became even more advanced and prevalent than Lemuria, and Lemuria began to shrink away.

Atlantis, eager and excited for new technology, developed at a rapid rate. They had connections with many extraterrestrials and exchanged different concepts and ideas for extraterrestrial technology and space travel. While still very spiritual, they had now become much more physical in their bodies. Although their bodies were different than today's, they were similar in many ways as well. They had government and many of the different concepts that you are developing today; they were well rounded and quite advanced. However, Atlanteans were advancing too quickly for their own good and ended up destroying themselves from their use of technology before they were ready for it. Electromagnetic energy caused a massive earthquake and flood, and Atlantis sank beneath the ocean. Many of the survivors were clones of original inhabitants.

Was there more than one Atlantean civilization?

Atlantis was spread out all across where your Atlantic Ocean is today — between the east coast of America and part of Africa. This was part of Lemuria at one time and then developed into Atlantis. There were several different civilizations over an expansive amount of time, thousands and thousands of years. There were three distinct growths that can be easily identified.

What were the high points of the Atlantean civilization?

They were extremely technologically advanced and were very eager to move ahead. They were also interactive with many different extraterrestrial life forms. A lot of spiritual development took place.

Besides the Great Flood, describe some of the low points of the Atlantean civilization?

They were moving ahead too fast without thinking of the consequences. They were too eager to advance and did not take time to think about what they were doing. They were also eager to push aside Lemuria and other civilizations — to be the top civilization at the time — and were getting too greedy and far from basic concepts of love and compassion.

Did the Egyptian civilization exist side-by-side with the Atlantean civilization or did it get started after Atlantis sunk into the ocean?

Egyptian civilization was one of the daughter civilizations of Lemuria existing at the same time as Atlantis. It was much smaller and did not develop as quickly as Atlantis did at the time, but ended up prevailing in the end.

Did Noah really build an ark and repopulate the planet when the Great Flood occurred?

The story of Noah is a lovely archetype for the repopulation of your planet. There were many beings who survived, taking many animals with them. But a distinct person who took two of every animal and repopulated the Earth is more of a story that incorporated the many people who survived the flood.

Did you say that the Atlanteans destroyed themselves with some sort of an electromagnetic accident or electromagnetic problem?

They got too consumed with their technology and power. The energy they were using from the Earth, combined with their extraterrestrial technology, created an earthquake that started the Great Flood, destroying and electrocuting their civilization.

Is that a possibility for our present civilization if we eventually develop, as Naor suggests, this idea of extracting energy from the electromagnetic fields of the Earth?

There are always possibilities to repeat the past. However, we hope that you'll be at a more advanced spiritual state of mind — a higher collective consciousness — eager to help your planet when discoveries about the potential of the Earth's energy are found. Right now, you are destroying your planet in different ways.

Are some of the people who are living in the United States today reincarnated Atlanteans?

Many are. They're all over the world, but there is a great majority reincarnated in America. Many have fallen into their old ways, but others are eager to work out their karma and create change for a better future.

Here on the Earth, people believe in marriage. What is the true meaning of marriage?

Marriage on your planet is two souls choosing to spend their Earth existence in physical time on your planet conjoined together. While it does have its benefits — and we hope that all souls and all beings have a soul to travel through the physical plane with — we see it falling apart, especially in your culture. So, we think that perhaps it's time that you find new ways for a lot of old traditions and work out new ideas that are more appropriate for the way that current life is going on your planet.

Do you believe that marriage is necessary?

We don't disagree with marriage in any way, but for two souls to love each other it does not need to be legalized or written on a piece of paper, and it does not seem to be working out in the same way as it has in the past. So, perhaps it's time for a change.

Do extraterrestrials marry their partners?

Many have life partners. We do not go through a church or a priest or have someone tell us that we love each other. Some of us have ceremonies and parties to pronounce our joint partnership. But, no, we do not have marriage in the sense that you do. And here on Pleiades we often have several different partners throughout our physical existence.

Do you think that gay people should be allowed to marry their gay partners?

We think that everyone should be able to love whomever they love and have the same rights as every other soul.

Many people on the Earth have low self-confidence. Is this caused by past lives or by how they were raised as children?

Both. The life they create in this present life often is a manifestation of karma from a past life and it can be externalized through a poor childhood or events that happen during childhood to create this low self-esteem, but it is usually planned out and executed for karmic purposes.

Are you saying that some people choose to live a life with low self-esteem for very specific learning purposes?

Indeed.

Do you see low self-esteem as a problem on the Earth?

Yes and no. Each person is on their own path working out their karma in the most appropriate way for them, and while we would like to encourage and bring up confidence in humanity, we are not going to change karma for people. We would like people to find their own power within themselves and bring it forth for the development and empowerment of humankind.

What can people do to raise their self-esteem and have more faith in their own godliness?

That is something that each being will have to come to terms with, but understanding that they *are* part of God and they *are* all part of the Source, and realizing that they do have a purpose and do have a point on this planet is important. Some beings on your planet have too much and could use some humbleness.

Why are some people good-looking? Where does their beauty come from?

When you look in the mirror, everything you're looking at is by choice. You chose everything about yourself before you came onto this planet. For karmic purposes, some people on your planet get wrapped up in your idea of beauty; others look past that. Many beings come back to Earth for karma associated with eating or food and for experiences that you do not get in all forms, and sometimes beauty can be overemphasized.

Is beauty an objective or subjective concept? In other words, is there a true ideal of beauty like a universal constant?

No. Beauty is different for *every* individual being, and everyone views beauty differently. And while many agree on certain objects or people as beautiful, they still see it differently, and what one might find unattractive another might find absolutely beautiful, and there is true beauty in that.

What draws us to beauty? Plato talked about mystical ideals that he believed existed in some other dimension, like an archetype of beauty. Perhaps we are drawn to this essence of beauty even if we are unable to clearly define it. Can you speak about this?

Beauty comes in many different forms, and perhaps being drawn to someone has nothing to do with their physical appearance, although you might think it does. It might have to do with their essence or their emotional being — how they project themselves on the planet, or their attitude. This can illuminate off of them, projecting beauty, attracting and bringing in this idea of beauty. It comes in many different forms on your planet and is different for all beings.

Is it possible for a spiritual master or human being to manifest a flower or other physical object out of thin air?

Yes. This art form has been lost for most of humanity. But with true devotion and true dedication to who you are as a spiritual being, you can create anything in any form.

Usually when humans manifest something it seems to take time from thought to creation, but I've read about spiritual masters who can manifest something immediately without a real time difference.

You, too, have this potential. It is an art form that takes true dedication and precise faith.

What are the rules or laws of manifestation?

In that form it takes true dedication and time, putting out and being exactly what you want to manifest, knowing with all truth and without any doubt that it will be manifested.

How does the manifestation actually occur? Do invisible spirits, such as devas and sprites, help with manifestation?

You draw in and create what you are manifesting, and so the particles that are necessary for what you are creating, with the correct intention and ideal purpose, will be magnetically drawn into you and your creation.

Is this something that the Pleiadians can do with relative ease?

We have that potential, but not many of us use it.

How many different types of invisible spirits live on the Earth?

There are an infinite number of spirits working around you constantly at all times. Different types of souls, light, spirits, and sprites are all working around you all the time.

Please discuss elementals such as sprites or nature spirits.

At the very beginning of your time on Earth, sprites interacted physically with humanity. They are still on your planet working within nature helping the flowers bloom and the trees grow, creating rain, snow, and ocean waves. They interact with nature, the elements, and animals. They stay within their elements and are kindhearted.

I thought the physical laws were responsible for things like rain and waves of the ocean. Are you saying that sprites influence the weather and plant life? Could you explain that some more?

Physical laws are to these elements as biology is to your body. There is a balance between soul, mind and body, and there is a balance between the sprites, the elements and physical laws.

What is the main purpose of the sprites?

Their dedication is to nature and the planet. They keep the plants growing, they keep the air as fresh as they possibly can, and they try to keep the water on your planet at a balance between the elements. Their job is becoming difficult as you destroy your jungles, deplete your atmosphere, and pollute your oceans. Your planet is becoming imbalanced and the sprites are having a difficult time maintaining it, but they will continue doing their job with the utmost patience for humanity.

Well, once again it's been a delight speaking with you. Thank you, Adam. Do you have anything else you'd like to share with us before we end today's session?

Thank you, I do appreciate it. We'll continue having these sessions. I'll see you soon. I bid you good eve. In love and light.

19

Greetings, it is I, Adam. How are you on this fine day?

Wonderful, thank you. Welcome, Adam.

I'd like to start off by talking about so-called demons that exist on your plane. They do not exist as demons. They are what you call angels who have fallen to your planet — choosing to incarnate as humans — to give up their status as angels to do work upon the Earth. In the Bible, they are thought of as demons or lost souls. They are not. They are actually achieving higher ranking, working towards more enlightenment. These many so-called fallen angels are among you each and every day. Some could use encouragement and a reminder to get back on an enlightened path towards the greater good.

May I answer some questions today?

How do we differentiate between these fallen angels and everyday people who are just making poor choices?

You can't, per se. These angels aren't necessarily making poor choices. They made the choice to give up their status so they could work among you, get hands-on experience, so to speak. While some of them have gotten wrapped up in the human experience, many of them have an internal instinct to help and to work towards the betterment of your planet. Many of them are working as teachers and guides in human form, and through interactions with them it can become clear who is not of human makeup.

This is a confusing idea. Why do you call them demons if they seem to be teachers or guides of some sort?

We do not call them demons. Many of your bibles and the Catholic religion think that angels who have lost their status become demons, for they think of Hell, although Hell is only upon your planet. So there is no such thing as demons, but the idea of a fallen angel is often referred to as that.

Are they associated with this concept of Satan or the devil, or even Lucifer, the fallen angel?

No, they do not associate with the dark side, although many of your people on the planet would think that would be the case, but it is not so, for there is no devil — there is none — only humanity's darker side.

So who was Lucifer?

Lucifer was created through imagination as a fallen angel who rebelled against God, and so he lost his status as an angel. However, it is only a story; Lucifer only exists in a reality in which you let him.

What about Satan or the devil? Are those just other terms for this concept of Lucifer?

Indeed. They are all part of the darker side of humanity. If you let them exist, they will, but only within a reality that you create. They do not exist in the greater good of all.

Would you say that these are projections of our own shadow nature, a psychological dynamic?

Indeed, for the polarities of humanity create good and evil, so they create a devil or a darker side, but it is not necessary.

So, when you started off today's conversation with this concept of demons or angels that have come to the Earth, was your main point to let us know that there are higher beings that made a choice — or even a sacrifice — to come down from the higher realms and assist humanity?

Indeed, that is exactly my point in this conversation.

I have questions about establishing enlightened societies on the Earth. What are the attributes of a successful, enlightened, conscious society? How do we get there from where we are today?

By making a conscious decision collectively that 1) you need change, that things are not going in the direction you had hoped, 2) collectively agreeing upon that change, and 3) being that change — not just wanting it, not just seeing it, but actually creating and being the change you wish to see, coming from a place of love and not necessarily from the brain. By including all beings on your planet, accepting them for who they are and the gifts that they bestow, and collectively working towards a better, more enlightened *collective* society that's more from a place of universal love and understanding instead of universal, monetary gain.

Again, how do we begin the process of getting there from where we are today?

By being that change and setting an example. You raise your vibration to the vibration you wish to see or be; match it up with that vibration instead of just wanting it or viewing it. Being it creates it. This will manifest it into your world. So, collectively by example with every interaction every day, setting the pace for change with new ideas and concepts that may seem radical at the time, you can create new dynamics for tomorrow.

Should we focus on developing our own higher consciousness or working within a group setting?

Does it have to be either one or the other? I think both are achievable and have potential for change.

Can you describe one or more enlightened patriarchal societies in human history?

Patriarchal societies, by definition, have male leadership creating male status over feminine status which throughout history has not worked very well. It has created an unequal connection between the sexes, so a more balanced society that is not patriarchal or matriarchal would be most achievable for you.

Have there ever been any successful matriarchal societies?

Indeed. There have been several indigenous matriarchal societies throughout Asia, Africa, and the Amazon. However, once again, having a matriarchal society is going to create feminine status over masculine status when you want to create a balance. So throwing away these old ideas, blurring the lines of what you know, and creating new ideas, new concepts totally outside the box that are different from the ones you already have, would assist your civilization to the greatest extent.

What is a healthy model of leadership for a new society?

Creating a new model by throwing away old ideas of governments and leaderships that already exist. Creating a new, balanced model, for obviously society is not working in the way that you wish it to. So, perhaps it's time for whole new ideas and concepts that don't exist yet, and a leadership that reigns from the heart, with love and compassion as a group dynamic.

Is leadership necessary?

That's something humanity will have to choose, but it is not necessary, per se. There are other ways for your culture to be. So you'll have to come to terms on whether you prefer leadership or some other type of joint dynamic.

How do we use our gift of co-creation to get from where we are today to where we want to go?

You can use all your gifts of humanity by recognizing them in yourself, seeing them in others, embracing the differences, acknowledging the similarities, and joining together to realize and influence change in your society, for it is achievable.

What tools can people use in a community setting to move toward higher collective consciousness?

Meditation — going within — is a universal tool that everyone can use to come to their own enlightened state of mind, and then together you can come to agreements for change.

What is peace? Is our human conception of peace limited?

Human conception of many ideas is limited by the Earth experience — but that is the Earth experience. Peace on your planet is coexistence without harm to one another; this is achievable. Each of you can reach this place of inner peace within.

Is this possible even when certain individuals on our planet are not interested in achieving peace?

At this time there are obstacles to overcome to reach that higher place, but over time it has the potential to be achieved, even with those individuals who are a challenge for your planet.

How can women be empowered?

By realizing that we are all equal — you are all of God — and there is no reason for women to feel like they are the lesser sex in any way. There is no lesser or greater; we are all One. We *all* can achieve whatever we desire to the greatest extent with true love and understanding.

Can you recommend any rituals or techniques for women during menstruation?

Connecting with their inner goddess and celebrating their existence as female in this life. Celebrating their choice to become female and be able to procreate and have the gift of pregnancy if they so choose. Celebrating it and embracing it during each monthly cycle is a ritual that they could use.

Please share your thoughts about the physical and spiritual significance of menstruation. Do you have any guidance on the menstrual cycle?

The menstrual cycle is one of the many connections that women have with *All That Is*. The flow with the Moon, with the ocean, with *All That Is*, is all connected. The choice to be female and have the experience of birth on your planet can be very spiritual and moving. You can embrace all of it and enjoy it — your menstrual cycle — and enjoy being female by celebrating it monthly. Meditating, perhaps under the Moon, could be very significant for the female.

How can we empower men?

Men on your planet have been in power for quite some time. However, we don't suggest letting women take over but making it equal, making sure that everyone holds the power, that it is equally distributed and not overly given to either sex. Everyone has the power; you are all connected with God.

It seems that we're not doing a very good job at raising boys in most of our cultures here on the Earth. What is it that we seem to be doing wrong and what is it that we could be doing differently to raise healthy boys into conscious, mature men?

You can change old ideas like these concepts that men have to be masculine and warlike and can't cry or show emotion. Throw away these old ideas for new ones, blurring the ideas about what's appropriate between genders. Realize that boys have a feminine side in them and females have masculine. Allow and encourage all children in each and every endeavor that they are most drawn to. Raise both boys and girls with love, understanding, and respect. Do not push them towards different ideas that you think, or that society thinks, are more appropriate for male or female. Do not raise them too quickly; give them their childhood. Let them learn and explore for themselves.

Are there any recommended rituals for men?

Men can celebrate their masculinity. While men naturally have more testosterone, instead of expressing it in anger or warlike ways, perhaps natural, friendly competition that men enjoy so much can help them celebrate their masculinity.

Please speak about parents who spank their children. Does that have an effect on violence in society?

We are not here to tell your society how to raise their children. However, society mirrors your actions, and so violence begets violence. Creating a chain of violence can cause that effect, so putting an end to that and learning how to discipline your children without physical harm in any way would benefit your society greatly.

Earlier, you mentioned power. What is power? How can humans heal our issues with power?

Power is energy; everyone has energy. Overabundance of power and too little power can become harmful in any situation. So finding a balance within your society, within individuals, within class dynamics of cultures — creating that balance of power so there is not too much in one direction and too little in another — is important. You can all find a mutual place to express that energy and express that power in a positive way towards creating good.

It seems as though some people on our planet have more power than others. Where do they get this power from?

You *all* have the power. Some use their power in destructive or inappropriate ways that creates this imbalance in your society. Others let their power wither away. So it appears that some have more and some have less, but you *all* have the power. Finding that balance, creating that balance, is a challenge that humanity will have to face.

Why do humans experience jealousy?

When you go to your planet and cross over the veil, you forget that you created the life that you're experiencing. So you often look to other beings and wish that your life or situation could be like theirs. Remembering that this is the life *you* created and that you can achieve whatever you wish in this life — you have the power to manifest it — and that everyone else is on their path that they created, can help in letting go of that envy and jealousy. Realize that it's not necessary; it's not an emotion that you need to feel.

Many people in relationships become jealous of their partners, fearful that they might be having sex or an emotional relationship with someone else. Can you speak about that for a moment?

Indeed. This is where the idea of non-attachment comes into play — having a healthy relationship in a healthy dynamic with your partner so that you have trust and understanding so there is no need for that jealousy. This also brings into play whether monogamous sexual partners in your society is most appropriate. Why are so many of your beings unfaithful? Perhaps it's time for change on this front as well.

What is the human ego?

Ego is the front that humanity has on the physical plane. Humans get wrapped up in concepts and emotions and these get mistaken for who you are. But the ego is just the cover that protects the soul; it can be pushed aside and not taken so seriously. So many humans are defensive of their ego; it can be hurt very easily. However, being non-attached — realizing that the ego can be let go of and does not need to be protected — can help humanity.

Is the ego a part of our nature or is it a type of figment? What is its intended purpose?

The ego is a figment and a part of human nature. It creates confidence within your physical form. But too much confidence and too big of an ego can create an unhealthy dynamic in the emotions of humanity.

Is the ego a part of our psychological nature?

It is part of your psychological nature as a human.

Is conflict bad? How can we transform conflict into something positive?

Conflict does not have to be negative. Conflict can jump-start change. As long as you don't let it get out of hand, and you recognize both sides and all parts of the conflict, you can achieve a higher level of change. So conflict does not have to be negative. Conflict can be positive if influenced in the right direction.

Do we have to suffer on the Earth? Is suffering necessary in order to develop true compassion?

Suffering does not have to be a constant on your planet. It can change, but at this point suffering is a major part of the karmic path — it creates compassion and understanding in humanity. Without suffering, the other polarity can only be understood in concept, not in reality.

How do we develop conscious decisions?

By coming from a place that's not of your ego. By coming from a place where you can step outside and look at both sides of every situation, where it's not necessarily for selfish reasons but for the greater good and for the good of humanity. Coming from that conscious place, not taking rash action, and coming from a place of love in every situation, can create a more conscious society.

Does a person's third eye need to be opened for them to achieve awareness and serve humanity?

It is not necessary to serve humanity through spiritual means in all situations. Many humans on your planet are creating change, achieving positive results, and helping humankind unconsciously or without any awareness of their spiritual existence. So it is not necessary for change.

How can people heal their relationship with money?

This is another obstacle that humanity will have to come to terms with: discovering what you want your relationship to be with money (and if you even want a relationship with money). Or, perhaps whether creating new concepts and ways for the development of your society and your civilization through money, trade, or different means is more practical for humanity. Coming to terms with the growth and changing of humanity where monetary needs and gain are reassessed.

I know several people on a spiritual path. Many of them seem to have problems accumulating enough money to manifest their spiritual dreams. Can you speak about that?

Indeed. When you are on the spiritual path you will be taken care of, even if it is in the most simplistic way where you're just getting by. But you will be taken care of, and if you continue down that path with the utmost faith and priority — where that is your entire priority, your entire existence — money loses its value.

I have a few questions about the Pleiadian lifestyle. Do Pleiadians pray?

We meditate daily, interacting and speaking with God within each of us, constantly. So in that way, yes, you could say we pray.

Do Pleiadians have any rituals?

We celebrate birthdays and diversity in love, like you do, and we even have certain holidays like you do, not religious in nature, but times to gather together and enjoy each other's company. In that way we have rituals.

What systems are in place on Pleiades to share the resources?

We use the energy within our planet as well as advanced technology that is beyond human conception at this time. We utilize, and do not destroy, our natural resources. The energy within our planet is used off our planet; we do not destroy any of our natural plant growth, air, or water.

Do certain Pleiadians oversee these functions?

The energy from our planet is constantly rejuvenating itself with a constant flow. We don't have any sort of production plant or anything that is keeping control of it, so it is not necessary for anyone to oversee it. It is constantly flowing and helping to resource our planet.

What is a typical Pleiadian diet?

We are mostly vegetarian in nature. We grow most of our own food individually and share different recipes and food. Some Pleiadians do eat meat. However, we do not farm and mass produce meat the way that you do. It would be, perhaps, a wild animal similar to your deer or elk that lived a full life and then every part of it is used — *if* they choose to eat meat, which not many Pleiadians do.

Do you have pregnancy like we do, and if so, how long are Pleiadian pregnancies?

We procreate in the same way as humanity, for we share similar genes. Our gestation is nine months as well.

Do Pleiadians experience anger, doubt or fear?

We have the capability to, but we choose not to. We hold ourselves at a higher vibration and choose to exclude those emotions — which you can do as well, if you choose to.

I know that we've spoken about this before, but could you please discuss it a little bit more once again? How do you educate your children?

We do not have school systems in the sense that you do. We teach through example, nature, and playing, and we let the children explore what they're most drawn towards. We let them experience their gifts and whatever crafts and ideas that they find interesting. If we have children who are interested in art, we let them experience that. If they change their minds and want to be astronomers, we encourage that instead. We let them achieve what they want to achieve and raise them in that way.

We started today's session talking about fallen angels that are here to assist the planet. Have any of them made a name for themselves on the Earth? Have any of them done anything spectacular?

Most of them go unnoticed. They live their lives cloaked in human skin doing simple tasks to help humanity. Many of them are influential teachers to your children. Many of them are helping feed people in third world countries. Others are helping spiritually in certain aspects, like shamans in South America. There have been ones that have achieved public notice, but that is not their point on your planet.

Are these angels aware of their angelic status or do they understand themselves to simply be of human nature?

They made the same sacrifice that you made coming to the Earth; they had to cross over the veil as well.

Thank you very much for coming through and answering our many questions. It's always a great honor and delight. Do you have anything else to share with us before we end today's session?

The honor's all mine. I will see you soon. In love and light. Many blessings.

20

Greetings. It is I, Adam. Today we'll start off by talking about the pure essence of *All That Is*. Although you started out as Light and will eventually return to it, the human concept and visualization of Light are extremely limited, for it is so much more. It is everything — concepts beyond your understanding at this time. Light makes up your pure soul. Your being is always returning to the Light, never to the darkness.

Feel the pure, Christ Light — where you truly are part of the Christ energy. Feel that energy, be that energy, spread that energy, marinate in that energy. Sharing and teaching, making others aware of their connection with the Light and *All That Is*, creating this awareness, this balance on your planet, is part of your mission.

May I answer some questions today?

Yes, welcome Adam. Did you peek at my questions? You started today's session by discussing Light and the pure soul. My first questions are about the soul and its evolution. You often begin each session with topics that are similar to my questions. Are you inspiring me with some of these questions when I'm preparing them for our sessions?

Indeed. We are connected.

Please summarize the evolution of the soul.

Evolution began from the Godhead — pure creative energy which manifested and actualized through change into Light, pure essence of being. This is not a light like a street lamp or a candle or even your Sun. This is pure essence of being. The only way to describe it in a human concept is "of the Light." And Light, through change, manifested itself into several physical forms — through plants, animals, humanity, extra-terrestrial — and it will continue until the ever-expanding universe boomerangs back and returns to the Light. The Light is connected with *All That Is*. All the humans, animals, matter, and energy are all connected. It is all part of you and is all part of God. It is all part of the soul energy.

Does the soul enter the human form for experiences or for some other type of evolution? Could you elaborate on that?

It enters into physical form for many different experiences that Earth has to offer that are only conceptual in soul or Light form. It also enters into physical form to create and use that energy to advance and bring along the evolution of change, for change is a constant that needs to be constantly manipulated and used. So, the billions of mini-Gods that you all are have creative instinct, and through physical form you can elaborate on the creative energy.

When somebody says, "I am feeling this" or "I am thinking of that," who or what is actually feeling those feelings or saying those words? Who or what is experiencing that within the physical body? Is that the soul?

That is the "I AM" essence. That is who you are. That is the Light. That is the demigod. That is the connection. I AM this. I AM that. YOU ARE. I AM.

Are we essentially souls, Light beings?

You are indeed creative Light beings in physical form.

Is there only one Godhead or are there multiple Godheads in other dimensions?

There are infinite Godheads and One, all in the same. It continues and is in *All That Is*. It is the pure, innocent, Creative Essence of the universe — *All One* and *All That Is*.

Will scientists ever be able to provide evidence confirming the existence of the soul?

As you move into a new Golden Age and the Christ energy illuminates your planet, the spiritual longing and the small reminders and inklings of your spiritual existence will spread across the globe. This concept and idea that is lost in passing onto your planet will then become more sought out and there will be proof in physical form of the "I AM" presence.

What is play or playfulness? Do all animals play?

Play is the physical manifestation of joy and ecstasy. It is very beneficial for humanity to continue playing into adulthood, taking time to have fun, to laugh, to enjoy each other. And yes, most animals' basic instinct is to play, but there are some that are more serious in nature.

What is the purpose of insects?

Insects are part of the circle of life on your planet. They help control the dynamic between humans, animals, and plants. While many of them seem like pests to humanity, they are just experiencing your planet. Recognizing that they have a point on your planet, not letting them affect you or your vibration, not being afraid of them or harming them, realizing that they are food to many of your animals and just letting them be, is best for humanity.

Do insects have an inner life?

Indeed, as do spiders, plants, and even rocks and minerals on your planet.

Do insects play?

Not in the sense that you are thinking of, but through mating rituals some insects interact in a playful manner.

Our bee colonies on Earth seem to be diminishing. Would you talk about this?

Indeed. This is related to the depletion of your atmosphere and the changing of the climate on your planet. It is of the utmost importance for humanity to start caring for your planet, your environment, for you are destroying it, and bees are part of that circle of life. They are part of the balance between nature and humanity; if they die off it will throw off humanity's balance as well. So paying more attention by coming up with solutions for a depleted atmosphere, dying rainforests, global warming, melting poles, and endangered species — all of which are connected — and helping to regain balance in nature will truly help humanity along in the future.

I have some questions about Damiana's inner experiences. When she was traveling with her third eye she visited or perceived of a universe with infinite strands of a twisted DNA-like grid. She felt really comfortable out there and laid down on it. What was that?

There is a biological makeup of DNA within the human body. With Damiana's imagination and concepts as a human, she visualized the universal body as being similar in matter and makeup and energy. So, through imagination she created the DNA of the universe, the grid pattern, which can be real through creation and manifestation.

Why did she feel so comfortable on it like she had already been there or done that before?

Because she has. Damiana has traveled the galaxies for many lifetimes. Her home is not of Earth origin. Her celestial travels remind her of times long ago and of the energy and essence of her soul existence.

Damiana also traveled to a world where she created anything that she wanted including other Light beings. When they started creating and clashing with each other she simply erased them so that they could start over. Please talk about this.

Damiana was experiencing creation in its most pure form, for you are creating every day. As souls — as part of God —

you've created your existence and you've created your physical plane and you've created this life, but it is forgotten and lost. She was experiencing this with her memory there, experiencing the beginnings of time branching off from the Godhead, creating a culture, a world, a civilization — and she gave them that creative power as well which she does not necessarily have control of, for she gave them free will. But she also decided she would begin again, for she was experimenting with this new concept of creativity in immediate form.

I have a few follow-up questions from earlier sessions. Naor said that Jesus manifested a man who looked like him, a doppelganger, and that *he* was crucified in place of Jesus. That seems like an important sacrifice or service for humanity yet this man was never formally acknowledged or honored. What can you tell us about this person? Where is the soul of this man today?

He is part of essence. He is not manifested in physical form at this time. His soul is connected with the Christ soul, as are many souls that experienced Jesus, many of the beings that he healed or took under his wing. That particular soul went on after that experience in that lifetime and lived a very pure and loving life, for he felt the Christ energy and continued spreading love. He had the choice to ascend like Jesus or continue reincarnating, which he did a dozen or so more times with different lives. Now he is working on the other side as a guide connected with many souls.

In an earlier session you said that we will influence change by changing concepts within ourselves making sure that all of who we are is complete. Please elaborate on this idea.

There are two different concepts here: 1) Creating change — taking the concepts and ideas that are on your planet that are seen as normal, that have been going on for hundreds or so years and throwing them out the window, starting anew, realizing that these are no longer working for your modern civilization, and 2) *Believing* that change within yourself and *being* that change. You manifest by *being* — changing your vibration to match up with the vibration you wish to create — for wanting only creates wanting, the longing effect, while *being* creates just that, what you are trying to create. So, *being* that change will create that change. Coming up with new concepts and ideas that are more appropriate for a modern, civilized, spiritual, all-inclusive society would best fit the dynamic of the human revolution ... evolution.

Was that a Freudian slip?

Perhaps.

Do civilizations on the Earth always become technologically advanced and then destroy themselves?

No. This has happened several times but it is a future of not learning from past experience. The Lemurians, for example, did not spend a lot of time focusing on technology. They were more interested in the spiritual aspect of their existence. Atlantis, however, was extremely technologically-based, and while this was one of their best attributes, it eventually caused their downfall. Modern civilizations today have this potential as well. We hope that you can help steer and teach through example another way so that your civilization does not repeat the same mistakes of the past.

Is our current fascination with technology positive or negative?

We think it is neutral. We think you are enamored with technology and moving ahead too quickly for your own good — with technologies that you're not fully aware of or in the right state of mind to properly use for appropriate purposes. There are still warlike thoughts and greed. Using this energy and technology for those purposes can destroy your planet.

Do you perceive that humans are out of touch with nature?

Many beings on your planet have lost touch with Mother Earth. They take it for granted and don't realize that by destroying it they're destroying themselves and a beautiful future for their children. We would like to see humanity realize their connection with the environment and with *All That Is*, help save it and become reconnected with nature.

Were some religions originally connected with nature? Is this a positive way to utilize religion?

There was a time on Earth when all beings were connected with nature. The elements were more pure and the elementals were prevalent; Mother Earth was cherished and honored. Returning to these roots through change and your connection with nature — spending time honoring it, loving it, experiencing it — and helping others to feel that love, the pure essence that nature provides, is what's important. Bringing humanity to a point where their values and ideas make a 180 degree turn, where there is love and compassion for your brother and your sister and your planet, while monetary gain and overabundance of power are realized as things of the past, are what's important.

Should humans be spending more time appreciating nature and protecting the environment?

We would love to see more humans protecting the environment, helping the animals, coming full circle — helping, loving, and being with nature — for you are part of nature.

How do we get people to understand that this is positive, not a movement backwards?

Through change within yourself and by example. By *being* that change, by *being* that person that's out loving and caring for nature and the environment. By helping humanity realize these concepts and ideas of what's important in today's society, the need to change, and that by destroying the environment for monetary gain you're only destroying yourself and a beautiful world for the future.

I have some follow-up questions on Atlantis. Earlier you said that some of the survivors of Atlantis were clones of the original inhabitants. Why did Atlantis create clones?

Atlantis was experimenting with many different types of DNA and biological aspects. They were combining different species' DNA, as well as cloning themselves. These beings were empty vessels for the most part and were mutant in nature. Atlantis was experimenting with aspects that in many ways present-day Grays are experimenting with, and it's destroying their civilization as well. Atlantis didn't know what to do with these biological advances that they were rapidly creating. They used these clones as assistants or slaves.

Did these clones get out of hand or were they always under the control of the Atlanteans?

They were very much out of hand, for without the "I AM" presence in them, just the biological makeup, they had only basic instincts with no compassion or emotion behind it. They became very destructive to themselves and to the Atlanteans.

Did Atlanteans experiment with cloning hybrids of humans and animals? What effect did that have on their civilization?

They did, and, once again, these were different mutant-like strains. While Atlantis was aware that they did not have Light-essence in them, they thought they could use them for assistance to do grunt work. But the clones and the hybrids had basic instincts. They rebelled against the Atlanteans, and many of the mutants were destroyed.

Did cloning always cause problems during Atlantean times?

Not always. Most of the clones were okay with their existence. After the Great Flood, many of the clones that continued on had a new start, so to speak. And while they were very basic and not extremely intelligent, they started a new life for themselves.

Did Centaurs truly exist at some time in history? What about unicorns?

During a time when the elementals were prevalent, centaurs, unicorns, dragons, minotaurs, and many different Earth element beings also existed. Some of your astrological symbols come from these different early Earth beings.

Centaurs are a hybrid between a human and a horse. That seems like something the Atlanteans would have tried creating.

The combinations that Atlantis created were mutant in nature. Centaurs and others lived during a time when gods ruled the Earth. It was a different planet then, not the Earth you see today.

Centaurs were associated with these gods?

Indeed, as were all that walked the Earth during that time. This is in many mythologies throughout your history.

Damiana's very first channeling a few months ago — a message that woke her up to memories of her soul identity and why she's here — was apparently from one of her friends during a lifetime in Atlantis. Could you provide more insight into this relationship?

Damiana has had several incarnations in different Atlantean times. She and Demetria were sisters in a particular lifetime. They lived on the water and communicated with many of the land mammals as well as the water mammals. She and her sister, Demetria, never married. They did everything together. They lived with the animals until a very old age when they both died a couple of days apart. We will have another session in the future discussing some of Damiana's important past lives on your planet as well as on other planets.

Thank you for another wonderful visit. Do you have anything else you'd like to share with us before we end today's session?

Thank you so much. Have a wonderful day. In love and light.

Human emotions are one of the many reasons that souls choose to incarnate on your planet, for not many planets share such a vast array of emotions. They are your connection, your empathy, with other beings — that link of understanding and relating to other people.

21

I bid you good day. It is I, Adam. May I answer some questions today?

Yes, hi Adam. How are you today?

I am doing quite well, thank you.

You seem to be doing better than Damiana. Today, she has a sore throat. Do you know anything about this?

Indeed. Damiana has held herself to a higher standard putting our words into practice, and so if she steps off the path a little bit she emotionally throws off the balance of her body. While taking our words and living them is important, it is not necessary for her to make herself sick. However, just being aware of it will help her heal.

I have questions about death. What happens when a person dies?

Death is only the beginning. It is change and transformation. It is not the end and can actually be quite a moving experience. Although many beings on your planet are sad and scared because they don't get to see their loved ones anymore, death is a release of the suffering and pain that can happen on your planet. When you die, you move into the astral plane and can manifest or create anything you wish. Or you can reincarnate back into an Earth body or a different physical body if you so wish. Or you can take some time off to help and do service on the other side of the veil.

It seems like the soul has many options after it dies. Does anyone help the soul make decisions?

Indeed. Some souls — old souls — are well versed in the death experience. When they pass away, they immediately remember all their lives, all their existence, and the non-limitations of the astral plane. Some souls are confused and do not understand. They realize that something has changed, but they aren't sure of exactly what. Many angels and ascended masters will assist them, helping them prepare for the afterlife or future reincarnations.

What exactly is an old soul versus a young soul? Does this mean that an old soul was created a longer time ago or does this mean that an old soul has just accumulated more awareness, more consciousness?

Souls are Light, and older souls have had more reincarnations. They have come again and again to the Earth plane and now are at a point of service towards humanity. And so, yes, their consciousness is more dedicated towards guidance and helping instead of just experiencing the experiences that are available. They are on a path of dharma more so than younger souls who are still working out their karma.

Can the soul be measured? Does it have any weight?

The soul has energy, and energy can be weighed. There is substance to the soul when in a human body. When free of the human body the soul can be weightless or the energy of the soul can be massive in weight, truly by choice.

What is fear?

Fear is a low vibration and many beings on your planet use it as a tactic for control. It is not necessary. You do not need to use fear in your life; you can raise yourself above it. There is nothing to be afraid of. You exist in every form and you will continue when you are no longer human. There is no reason to be afraid, for fear only leads to more fear, so letting it go, realizing everything is a passing moment, every situation will change, will help in not letting it bring you down.

Is fear associated with pain? Here on the Earth, people would like to avoid pain.

Fear can be associated with pain, but non-attachment to that pain or that suffering releases the fear. Not holding on to it, realizing that pain is a part of the Earth experience and letting it go, releasing it, is possible. There are many masters who have achieved status of non-physical pain where they no longer physically feel pain on your planet. This is by non-attachment to it, releasing themselves from fear, and holding themselves at a higher vibration where fear and pain do not affect them.

Do animals and insects experience fear?

Indeed. Animals and insects, both, can experience fear. I'm quite sure that it is terrifying for the fly that gets caught in the spider web, but its death will be quick and it will be released from its fear in no time.

Do plants experience fear?

Plants do not experience fear in the sense that humans and animals do. They are neutral in emotions, so they do not feel fear or pain or even joy and ecstasy in the way that you do. However, they are connected and do know the difference between happiness and sadness, positive and negative energy.

When humans kill animals for their meat, if the animals experience fear when they are being killed, is that fear energy transferred to those who eat the meat?

Indeed. Mass production in the raising of farm animals by humanity is not appropriate. The negative energy of these empty lives that you have given the animals — plus the destroying of your planet due to this mass production — is transferred into that meat, as well as hormones that are not healthy for humans. If humanity chooses to continue eating meat, honoring the animal and letting it live a full life is the most appropriate way.

Regarding fear, there is an extraterrestrial group that some people are concerned about. Please discuss the Grays.

The Grays have visited with humanity for thousands of years. They have extremely advanced technology that they have exchanged with your government so that they can perform science experiments on the occasional human and animal on your planet. They lack human emotions and have cloned themselves into a nonsexual race where they are now asexual and are dying off, so they will occasionally abduct humans to try to recreate their sexual reproduction. The Grays are the extraterrestrials that landed in Roswell years ago (and elsewhere on Earth throughout your history). They are not evil, per se; they just don't share the same emotion and compassion that many humans, and some of us extraterrestrials, have. Their technology is far advanced, even more than ours.

Did you say that the Grays have technology that is more advanced than Pleiadian technology?

Indeed. The Grays spend most of their time developing higher technology, for that is where their priorities lie.

What exactly do they do when they abduct human beings? Do they take them onto their ships? Do they perform operations?

Both. Sometimes they abduct, do experiments, then return the human being; the person will have no recollection, or in some instances will dream about it. There have been cases where they have permanently taken a person with them. You need not be afraid, for it is not part of your path or energy, and the Grays have no need for you. We protect and look over you. The people that they do abduct have made this agreement before coming onto the planet. Their energy resonates with the Grays, so it is ideal for the Grays to abduct them.

Are there any lasting effects on the people who have been abducted or is it mostly an innocuous experience, one where they just continue on with their lives?

In some cases. There are cases where it destroys their sexual organs or sexual appetite, or other times when it boosts their sexuality. Some also become more advanced and intelligent from the experience. Others don't recognize any difference, or may only have a vague sense that something is different.

Are the Grays also responsible for cattle mutilations?

In many cases, yes. They also take dogs, cats, elk, bears, different animals. They will take organs and different body parts of these animals for experiments and for advanced knowledge, for there is much of Earth that they don't understand.

Did you say that our government made an agreement with the Grays allowing them to do this in exchange for certain technology?

Indeed. You have advanced very quickly in the last few decades. This is partly due to the exchanges with the Grays.

Where are the Grays from? Do some of them currently reside here on the Earth?

The Grays have a planet. However, most Grays no longer inhabit it. Most Grays are space travelers; they have several different groups that are spread out across the universe. Some Grays reside within your Area 51, as well as within your Russian and Korean governments.

Are they third-dimensional beings?

The Grays can be third-dimensional beings, but they are mostly fourth-dimensional. They go back and forth between the third and fourth dimensions.

Please talk about the Bermuda Triangle.

It contains an electromagnetic energy field that is extremely strong. It is a whirlpool of energy, and often when technology passes through that region it becomes scrambled for a period, or destroyed. This is just the electrical-magnetic whirlpool effect.

This electromagnetic energy resonates throughout your planet, but at that particular spot it boomerangs back within itself and creates this whirlpool "back and forth effect" that mixes with the technology passing through.

Is the Bermuda Triangle related to Atlantis?

Yes, Atlantis spread out over that same area and Atlanteans were experimenting with this electromagnetic energy. When the Great Flood happened, pushing them under water, it created this whirlpool's electromagnetic effect where the energy got trapped in that area.

I have a couple of questions on human sexuality. Teenagers seem to be having sex at younger and younger ages. Do you see this as a positive development or a problem?

This is one of the many challenges, and choices through change, that humanity is going to have to deal with. It is one of the many areas where humanity should look at with new ideas. We think that since teenagers are so prevalently sexual that perhaps a different format for the mass rearing of the children from more developed, older beings may be more appropriate. Also, learning to channel that energy for other purposes, besides sexuality, would most benefit humanity. More sexual education for these teenagers would also benefit humanity so there aren't so many young parents.

With the rise of the internet, pornography has proliferated and become easily accessible to everyone, including young teenagers. Is this stimulating sexuality before its time?

Your *society* is stimulating sexuality before its time. You have a rather sexed-up culture. They put a lot of emphasis on sexual energy. This energy, while sexual in nature, can be channeled into more appropriate avenues. Toning it down and not putting so much emphasis on sex in your culture would benefit humanity greatly.

Is part of the reason that humanity appears to be in a phase of hyper-sexuality because we are liked caged rats under great stress and need to release the tension?

Sexual energy is one of the few energies that humanity has attained, and instead of working on a better avenue for that energy, humanity immediately wants to release it. It has become a fixation in your society. Throughout your culture there is a huge focus placed upon sex and sexuality. You wonder why many children are having sex earlier and your society thinks it's a problem, but they are throwing this sexuality into their faces. The children are immediately surrounded with this sexual energy.

Please provide your perspective on the ramifications of abortion.

We think that it is the choice of the mother, for there are circumstances where it is not appropriate to bring a soul into a negative situation. While there are many souls who wish to enter into the Earth plane, they understand when a mother makes that extremely difficult choice, and they will make their reincarnation when the timing is right. However, we do not think abortion should be used as birth control. We do think more sex education for these teenagers — these young kids who are having sex — is important, for that sexual energy *is* there and they should know how to protect themselves.

Do you consider abortion a form of murder?

We don't think anything is black or white. There are lots of gray areas in these types of situations. There are circumstances where we think it is the best choice for the soul coming in, and for the mother, that they do not go through with the pregnancy. Of course, there *are* situations where it is not the most appropriate line of action. But abortion in general we do not consider murder, and we do not judge the young ladies who have to make that difficult decision.

Do people who have abortions create karma that needs to be balanced?

Every situation creates karma, whether labeled good or bad. Learning and growing from it can help resolve that karma.

Do you think that our current birth control methods are adequate? Are they too disruptive to the female hormonal system? Do Pleiadians use birth control?

We do agree that some of the birth control on your planet is disruptive to the natural cycle of the female, but it is important to have these choices *and* to develop a more natural remedy of birth control. On our planet, many of the females monitor their cycle and are aware of when they are most fertile and when it is okay to engage in sexual acts. That is how we most often control our births. Also, we are not overly abundant with our sexual energy. While we enjoy having sex, it is not all the time. We often use that sexual energy — and many different energies — for other purposes.

Is capital punishment ever justified? Is there ever a good reason to kill another human being?

Again, we don't look at things as black and white. There are many gray areas to all situations. We don't think death is necessarily the answer for punishment, but we are not going to tell you what's right or wrong. This is another one of the many different situations that humanity is going to have to come to terms with and agree upon. We do see within the next 100 to 200 years, humanity getting to a place of higher enlightenment where murder and war are things of the past.

Is self-defense a good reason to kill another person?

Every situation is different. Having set rules when every situation is different does not seem like the most appropriate way to go about things. Looking at each individual situation and coming up with the best results or punishment or resolution for that situation may be a better option.

If a violent person broke into someone's home and threatened a man's wife or child, do you believe the man of that household would be justified in using deadly force to stop that intruder from harming his family?

Again, it depends on the situation as every situation is different. However, if that intruder is harming the family or going to harm the family and there is no other way to stop him, perhaps it might be justified.

Can wars be justified? For example, did Hitler need to be stopped?

Your civilization justifies wars every day. However, again, every situation is different. And, yes, Hitler did need to be stopped. So of course there *are* situations where a plan of action is necessary. A nonviolent plan of action should be considered first, however, and if there are no other choices, then, yes, war can be justified.

Please discuss the widespread violence in Mexico.

The drug wars and violence in Mexico are cultural karma from Mayan and Aztec civilizations. They are now working on their karma and clearing their karmic slate.

What can we, as a planetary civilization, do to help nations such as Mexico with their out-of-control violence?

You can realize that they are working out their karmic slate and you can work on *your* purpose in this lifetime, leading by example, helping to uplift the energy in every situation. You can create a loving and compassionate dynamic leading by example, having compassion for those who *are* undergoing these more difficult karmic choices. And as a society you can come up with a best plan of action to assist without interfering with their karmic slate, helping them to come to a more uplifting place, making better choices.

When you say that we can "assist without interfering with their karmic slate," I know that you don't mean that we should just allow the violence to continue. Do you mean that we should be setting up a plan that helps the Mexican government to deal with this problem?

That is a plan of action that will have to be humanity's to make. But, yes, assisting government, coming up with positive choices without taking over and making those choices for them — working side-by-side, but not for them.

We want to do everything in our power to stop the violence even though, as you say, some of these killings are some sort of karmic balance.

The killings are a balance. But leading them by example and doing your purpose, helping alongside their government rather than overtaking it, is in everyone's best interest.

What is a good method to resolve conflict between opposing groups to create peace on Earth?

Compromise — letting go of the will and the ego and coming to a resolution between both sides. Finding out what both sides want and creating a positive resolution, an agreement where it can be a win-win situation. Not undermining or overlooking what one group wants. Giving them both time and compassion.

Thank you for coming through today. As always, we enjoy your presence and appreciate your words of wisdom.

Thank you. I bid you good day. Many blessings. In love and light.

22

Good morning. It is I, Naor. May I answer some questions today?

Yes, hi Naor. I have some questions about Damiana's experience yesterday. She traveled with her third eye to a beautiful, golden room with several ascended masters. Where was that?

That was one of the many private locations the masters have upon your planet. That particular retreat was located not far from the Himalayan Mountains. The energy illuminating there was to help rejuvenate and purify Damiana's channel as she moves further along this path. She can visit there again whenever she likes.

To get there, Damiana traveled up in an elevator. She felt like she was in some heavenly region. Are you saying the retreat was actually located somewhere on the Earth?

It's off the Earth, but located above your Himalayas. It's in another dimension just outside Earth's atmosphere.

Was the elevator a visual tool that Damiana used to get there or that the ascended masters used to bring her there? How does that work?

Indeed, it was something relatable to humans. And so, through the power of thought and imagination — a combination of Damiana's and the masters' intentions — the elevator was conceived as a tool to bring her there.

Once inside the retreat, Damiana saw pictures of ascended masters on the wall, but they seemed to be alive. Please talk about that.

In other dimensions there are no limitations. While many of the masters weren't physically present at the time, they left part of themselves there to greet Damiana and make her feel safe in their retreat in the sky.

Damiana floated on a rejuvenating pool of water. What was that?

This was energy to help open up and clear her vessel, helping along this path, giving her energy and confidence within the channel. She can go there whenever she likes to regain energy and confidence.

An outline or copy of Damiana left her body that was floating on the water and it traveled elsewhere in the universe. What was that about?

This was more experimentation with Damiana's will and third eye, as well as one of the non-limitations of these other worlds where she can stay and rejuvenate *and* go exploring at the same time.

Damiana's copy traveled to a planet of crystals and prisms with bright lights and colors shooting out in all directions. What was that planet?

That was one of many planets of light — light in its purest form enjoying just being as it illuminated around the planet and duplicated itself through prisms and crystals. There are many planets throughout the universe where light exists within itself. Some of them are similar to that one and others are very different. She can see more in the future.

When Damiana's copy returned to her body that was floating in the bath, she noticed that her chakras were floating just above her. She pulled them in one at a time. What was happening there?

They were rejuvenated. The energy within them was balanced and she herself had been balanced. So she was able to observe it in this world, bring them in, feel the balance, and get out of the bath.

When Damiana came out of the rejuvenating bath there was an elixir waiting for her. She drank it and felt high energy, but she quickly returned to Earth. What was the elixir and why did she return to her physical body so quickly?

Yesterday's experience for Damiana was to rejuvenate her energy and clear her channel. While her experience was of the utmost benefit, the elixir was just finishing off the job and bringing her back to Earth, giving her a quick rejuvenation and returning her to the physical plane.

I have some questions about chakras. What are chakras?

The chakras make up the energies, or energy orbs, of your physical body. Each chakra in the ideal physical body should be balanced. There are many ways to consciously be aware of these chakras and balance them. They are on the physical body going up from the base of your spine to the tip-top crown of your head. You can physically feel them by placing your hand in the center starting between your hips. You can feel a different energy about three or four inches up the spine in the middle of your body. The chakras only exist in the physical body. In your soul existence or in your Light existence the energy radiates constantly. You can balance the chakras through daily meditation, through yoga (which centers them), and through breathing exercises.

Are the chakras actually in the physical body or are they in some energetic realm?

These different, separate centers of energy are in the physical body but they are not of the physical body. These energies combine and make up your soul existence. In the physical body, you can feel them as they feel different than your normal physical skin.

Are there only seven chakras or are there smaller energy centers elsewhere in the body?

Indeed. There are chakras that illuminate off these main chakras, and there are ones existing off your body, around your body, as well. But if you get the main ones balanced, the others will follow along.

How else can people discover which of their chakras need to be opened or balanced?

Through physical ailments, often, or through physical pain as well. Sickness of the stomach often throws off chakras. A sore throat like Damiana had for the last several days caused her throat chakra to become off balance. After her bath yesterday, she is fully aligned.

What exactly is the purpose or function of the throat chakra?

Communication — being able to speak up when most appropriate and to not speak when not appropriate. To hold back in petty arguments or stand up for yourself when you are being oppressed. The throat chakra is a rather important chakra and you use it every day.

What is the Kundalini energy? Is it related to the chakras?

Indeed, but Kundalini energy is another word for the sexual energy that radiates throughout your body. Many beings on your planet release this energy through sex. However, you can harness this energy and use it for spiritual awakening and pure energy. It does not have to be released in a sexual manner.

Please discuss the different purposes of the third eye and crown chakras.

The third eye chakra is for clairvoyance — visiting and seeing other worlds. The crown chakra is for higher communication with guides, with ascended masters, with God, with your higher Self. It's the connection that's made.

When Damiana travels with her third eye, is she actually leaving her body or is that something different?

It's different. She's traveling with her third eye, but she is not leaving the body in the sense of an "out of body experience" or "near-death experience." She is physically here in presence while visiting other worlds through her mind's eye.

I know that she's physically present, but it's still unclear to me whether or not her consciousness is actually leaving her physical body. Is that related to the third eye?

Indeed. Her consciousness is viewing other worlds through her third eye and visiting in that sense. In a way, she is bringing those worlds here to her consciousness instead of the other way around.

When Damiana travels with her third eye, for example when she visited Pleiades, she seems to have some sort of a physical or etheric body that she brings with her. Can you talk about that?

Indeed. She does create herself into an ethereal body, but this is only for experiential purposes. And, again, she's bringing these worlds to her, not the other way around.

Is it possible for her to go *there*? I don't understand. It seemed as though she was actually on Pleiades.

Yes. She is experiencing these planets and these worlds, but she is bringing them to her third eye. She is experiencing them through a clairvoyant vision. So she is truly experiencing them, but she is creating them here. It's very confusing, I know. As Damiana develops this gift and continues experimenting and using her third eye, these concepts will become more clear.

The crown chakra is not used for astral traveling, is that correct?

Indeed. The crown chakra is your connection to *All That Is* — to your higher Self, to God, and to everyone.

What is the silver cord that I've read about and does it truly exist?

The silver cord is a metaphor for life and, yes, life does exist.

I've heard that when people leave their bodies and travel elsewhere, there's a silver cord that tethers them to their physical body.

The silver cord that you're speaking of is just part of the life force. Many people visualize and create it into the silver cord. It connects them to their body so they don't permanently leave it. Some people visualize this silver cord and some do not.

What are human emotions?

Human emotions are one of the many reasons that souls choose to incarnate on your planet, for not many planets share such a vast array of emotions. They are your connection, your empathy, with other beings — that link of understanding and relating to other people, feeling the many emotions there are through a connection with humanity.

Do humans have an emotional body? Is it different from the emotional chakra located near the solar plexus?

Your body can feel and connect to these emotions. It is only through experience on Earth that you can comprehend and relate to these emotions, for in the astral world and in soul experience these emotions are understood but not experienced; they are just concepts. On Earth, you create this emotional body that you speak of and experience these emotions in the purest form. Solar plexus has become the chakra that is known to relate to the emotions. However, it is not the only chakra related to emotions. The base chakra and sacral chakra are where jealousy comes from. The heart chakra is where love and happiness come from. So there is a wide array of emotional expression between your chakras.

Do humans actually possess emotions or do they flow through us?

That is truly up to you, for many humans hold on to, manifest, and become an emotion, but it is not necessary. You can simply let it go if you so choose.

What is the best way to work with emotions?

Experience them. Enjoy the higher ones, release the lower ones, and go into every situation without preconceived emotions. Also, don't hold on to them for too long.

Where do the emotions come from?

They come from basic human instinct and your connection with each other — relations and relatability.

I have some more questions about the etheric body. Do humans have a non-physical, etheric body?

Yes, however many of the humans have forgotten about it. In your dreams each and every night, your etheric body turns to the astral world and explores. This etheric body is very real. You can consciously separate them during meditations as well.

You can separate the etheric body from the physical body?

Indeed.

What is the purpose of the etheric body?

The etheric body is your connection to the astral world and the universe so you are not stuck in this physical plane through your whole physical existence. There is still that connection to the etheric world which you came from. This is why sleep is so important for humans. It's important to make those connections at night and go back to your etheric world.

I can't see the chakras on my physical body in the same way that a surgeon can see and describe physical organs, so it seems to me that chakras are in the etheric body. However, you said that they are in the physical body.

They are in both, but in the physical body they are separated into these energy centers. In the etheric body they are all connected, they are all one, there are not seven chakras; there is just one, big energy ball. But in the physical body you can physically feel these chakras if you so choose.

Is the etheric body related to the third eye?

It can be, but in a different way. In your dreams you travel in your etheric body and your third eye is connected as well. When Damiana travels with her third eye, she creates her etheric body and places it in these worlds.

I have some questions about mythology. Did the mythological gods truly exist and visit the Earth?

There was a time when the mythical Greek and Roman gods actually existed on your planet. It was in a different dimension. It was a different time and a different planet at the time; it was a world of the gods. These mythological archetypes still exist and have consciousness within the universe today.

Adam said that centaurs, unicorns, dragons and minotaurs really existed side-by-side with elementals at some time in history. When did this occur? Were they third-dimensional, physical beings?

No. They, too, were in another dimension and they existed thousands of years ago on your planet. It was also a different planet at that time. The elementals still exist on your planet today in another dimension. They are working extremely hard every day to try and rejuvenate the destruction that the humans have caused on the planet.

How did the Greeks know about the mythological gods?

The Greeks connected just like we are, through channeling. They had several oracles at the time and they connected with many gods and many beings from the other side.

I have some questions about cause and effect. Is everything related by cause and effect or are some events related in a non-causal manner?

Everything is from cause and effect. Everything that you put out, you will get back; it is a universal law.

Karma is obviously cause and effect but some things seem to be linked in a synchronous manner without a cause and effect relationship.

One that you can't physically relate to, but everything in the universe is cause and effect (or what you're calling cause and effect). Everything that you put out, you get back. And so, creation is cause and effect related.

What about astrological correlations? Do the planets actually *cause* certain events in a person's life or do they simply happen simultaneously?

They mirror your choices so that what you put out, you get back. It may seem like it's cause and effect on the planets, but it is truly cause and effect on *your* part being mirrored by universal expression.

Will Damiana ever have an opportunity to visit your home planet?

In due time, yes, in due time.

Today, you seem to be speaking in some sort of a foreign accent. What is that about?

Damiana and I are more connected and so some of my natural speech tones are coming through today. After yesterday's rejuvenation bath, Damiana's vessel is a little more clear and we — myself, the Pleiadians, ascended masters, and the others — hope to be coming through more clearly in the future.

Do you have anything else you'd like to share with us before we end today's session?

Thank you; the pleasure is always mine. I do appreciate it. I'll be back again. Many blessings. In love and light.

The Council of Intergalactic Relations is a branch of the Extraterrestrial Council that was established by benevolent extraterrestrials in the galaxy who share a passion for moving forward to create a more dynamic and beautiful future for all who exist within the universe. We regulate and monitor interactions between different extraterrestrial races and watch over and protect many planets.

23

Good afternoon, it is I, Adam. Today we'd like to start off by discussing something that might get a little confusing. It's a bit different than what we've discussed in the past. As the Earth is moving into a new dimension, you thought you were going into the fourth dimension. However, *density* and *dimensions* are different; you are moving into the fourth *density*. You are actually moving into the *fifth* dimension, if you want to get technical. What is the fifth dimension, you ask? It is the dimension of love. Humans are moving into this higher, more adaptable, relatable consciousness that can expand across your globe. It is a universal love, a pure and all-inclusive love.

May I answer some questions today?

Yes, welcome. Thank you for visiting. Today, you've introduced this idea of density. Please elaborate on that.

Density and dimensions both have to do with vibrational energy. When people speak of *dimensions,* most often they are actually referring to *density* and moving into this higher density. You are in third density moving into fourth density. When you have your second birthday, you're actually going into your third year of life; this is very similar in concept. So, density and dimension have somehow gotten blurred together. They both are associated with this higher vibration of the planet, but we wanted to make clear this new concept.

Well, you've made it "clear" by confusing us. How does this relate to frequency?

I do understand how this can be confusing. This is why we waited until now to bring up this concept. Frequency is the speed and energy that the vibrations are moving at. These different frequencies create the higher or lower density within the dimensions.

You said that we're moving into a higher density. I think of density as something similar to mass, so when you say "higher" density it has an opposite connotation. Do you understand my confusion with that?

Indeed. Higher with less density, as in a higher frequency creating lower density.

I'm still confused about the difference between, let's say, fourth density versus fourth dimension, or fifth density versus fifth dimension.

Fourth density relates to fifth dimension in the same way that second birthday relates to third year of life. They are two and the same with different labels for understanding. There is not much difference but some confusion when people say you are moving into the fourth *dimension*. You are actually moving into the fourth *density*.

So, technically we're now in the fourth dimension moving into the fifth dimension?

Indeed, for you are mastering time which is the challenge of the fourth dimension and third density.

I don't know if we're mastering time, but we're sure experiencing it in a linear sense.

Indeed. It is a limitation of this density, and Earth has experienced it.

Let's use today's topic to segue into extraterrestrial beings that exist on other planets, perhaps in other densities and dimensions. For example, we've been talking with Naor who is supposedly from the fifth dimension. Does this mean that he's really from the fifth *density* and *sixth* dimension? And are you Pleiadians not of the *seventh* dimension? Are you really from the seventh *density* and *eighth* dimension?

Exactly. We are indeed actually of the eighth dimension in those terms. In reality, these are all just terms to create relatability in different groups and frequencies. They're just labels though, and they really have no meaning besides the meaning you give behind them. We are just clearing up the blurred line between these two definitions.

Are these densities and dimensions going to progress whether we choose it or not? How does that relate to our free will?

The energy is already there and is heading in that direction. Change will happen no matter what. Adapting to it and going with it, instead of fighting it, and assisting others in this time of change, will benefit your planet greatly.

Today I'd like to ask about some of the different extraterrestrial groups. Please talk a little bit more about the Alpha Centaurians.

The Alpha Centauri are a strong and confident group. They have a tough exterior with a noble heart. They are one of your many protectors. They also protect many other beings in the universe. They stand up for justice, representing free will and fairness. They work with us and share their strong-willed vibrations throughout the universe.

Do they actually reside in the region of Alpha Centauri? Are they in our dimension or another one?

They are in a higher dimension, the same one as us. They can relate to all dimensions beneath them, however, and for your understanding they do indeed reside in the area of the Alpha Centauri stars, as we reside in our dimension near the Pleiadian stars.

Is their DNA makeup different from ours?

Indeed. They are in physical bodies that are different biologically. They have also mastered the separation of the physical and spiritual (or etheric) bodies, if they so choose, being able to separate them at will. And while they rely on their physical bodies, it is their lightning quick, sharp minds and logic that help them assist other beings — bulk and brains.

Are their physical bodies similar to third-density (or fourth-dimensional) bodies on the Earth? Or are their bodies relatable to the densities and dimensions in which they exist?

It is a body within their dimension, not within yours.

How do the Alpha Centauri reproduce? Is it similar to humans and Pleiadians?

They do reproduce through sex and emotional connections that are made between loving partners. It is similar to you and us, yet different.

Please speak about extraterrestrials known as the Arcturians.

The Arcturians have worked with us *and* humanity for many, many years. They are universal healers connecting with many shamans, spiritual healers, priests and priestesses of your planet. Their healing power is some of the greatest within the universe, for they resonate so high and fast, with such pure intention, that they manifest only the purest of energy.

Do they actually heal humans or do they work with our healers to guide them to become more proficient at healing?

Both. They will often heal starseeds who are ailing. They also work with many healers on your planet assisting them through telepathic communication.

Please speak about the group of extraterrestrials from Sirius.

Sirians do share some of humanity's DNA, and ours as well. They are in many ways your future, if the energy continues on in the direction that we see it heading. They have a soft spot for you humans as well, for they have been where you were and rose above it. They came out on the other side with such positive energy and vibrations. They are very technologically advanced and are quite the space travelers, exploring all the different nooks and crannies of the universe.

Are they higher dimensional beings as well?

They are just a step ahead of you in the fourth density, fifth dimension.

In an earlier session you said that the *Pleiadians* represented our future. Does it depend on choices humans make as to whether we'll move closer to the Pleiadians or the Sirians?

In a way, we are both your future — Sirians being somewhere down the line and the Pleiadians being further down that line — if the energy heads in the direction that we see it heading.

How often do Sirians interact with beings upon the Earth?

There are telepathic communications with Sirians every day. Many starseeds have come from Sirius. They reconnect with their brothers and sisters through channeling, or telepathic, intergalactic communication.

Has there ever been physical interaction between Sirians and humans?

Indeed, for your governments have interacted with them and discussed an intergalactic council which would include Earth within it. The Sirians have discussed this with your governments and realized the timing is not quite right yet. During Lemurian, Atlantean, and ancient Egyptian times, the Sirians freely came and went, with trade upon your planet.

What sort of trade? What were they interested in on the Earth?

Sharing futuristic technology as well as spiritual concepts and ideas, and giving guidelines for different energies of your planet as well as energies within each other.

Which extraterrestrial groups have actually communicated with our government?

Quite a few, actually. With high hope, the Council of Intergalactic Relations has opened up to your government to help it rise above itself and heed warnings so as not to repeat the past. The Grays, of course, have shared their technology in exchange for the spare human and cattle every now and then. The Reptilians have even made contact with your government. And while your government did give in to the Grays, they did not give in to the Reptilians.

When you say that extraterrestrials have been in contact with our government, do you mean our legitimate government — the one elected by the people — or do you mean some sort of a shadow government?

Both. Many of your past presidents have made contact with extraterrestrials, although your present-day one has not. However, these shadow governments are the ones that most often work with UFO technology and extraterrestrials.

Please talk about extraterrestrials from Andromeda.

We are extremely aware of this extraterrestrial group, for they are a branch of Pleiadians that have gone a separate way. We, too, have had our past conflicts to overcome, and not all Pleiadians were in agreement, and so many thousands of years ago they started their own civilization. Thus, this particular group, while similar in biological makeup, is very different in spiritual energy and their connection to *All That Is*. They are similar to humans in their connection to material and physical needs. They are never far from our hearts but they choose a different way of life.

Do some of the extraterrestrials from Andromeda communicate with people on the Earth to provide any kind of spiritual guidance? Or do you think that their guidance wouldn't necessarily be of the highest caliber?

It happens occasionally, for like Earth they have individuals who are more spiritual and seeking of answers. But not many of them are at a point of sharing.

The Reptilians have a scary reputation. Would you please talk about them once again?

Indeed. The Reptilians are quite scary. They always have the intention of harming and harvesting humans for food, for they are extremely aggressive and even cannibalistic. They are quite set, focusing on their will and ego. They do not share emotions or care for other beings in the universe. They will not reach Earth, however. The Alpha Centauri and Pleiadians protect you.

How did the Reptilians communicate with our government?

With our permission and protection and assistance, they have come to your planet and talked face-to-face. They have also communicated telepathically to your government. And, in fact, there are reincarnated Reptilians on your planet.

That was going to be my next question. Is there a large contingent of humans on our planet that are actually reincarnated Reptilians?

There are some. Not a lot, but quite a few working on the shadow side of the government and some of the large corporations that are destroying your planet, for if they can't have you or control you, they'd rather just destroy you from the inside out.

You said that some of the Reptilians were communicating telepathically with certain people. Who channels the Reptilians?

Other reincarnated Reptilians within your shadow government. Even some pure channels with the best intentions don't realize who they are channeling. They don't protect themselves and reach for the highest truths, and this low vibrational energy could come through in disguise.

You said that the Reptilians were kept from coming to the Earth by the Alpha Centauri and Pleiadians. However, it sounds like there was an exception where you allowed them to speak directly with our government. Is that correct?

This is true. With our assistance and supervision there have been exceptions made.

Are there any other extraterrestrial groups that you think would be important for us to know about at this time?

You have mentioned quite a few of the most positive. There are also the Essassani, as you know, and the Ashtar Command, as you know, as well as a few others that over time will make their presence known. But continuing to work with us, as well as Naor, brings us the greatest joy, for the potential to help humanity through this transition, bringing you to a higher consciousness, to a better place of love for all, and letting you stand up for yourselves while establishing a grand civilization for other extraterrestrial civilizations to look to as an example, is our goal. We wish only the best for humanity.

Damiana channeled Naor the other day and he spoke with an accent. Today, you're speaking through Damiana without an accent and it seems like there's a pretty good connection. I'd like to get your perspective on Damiana's recent experience at the ascended masters retreat. Also, will Damiana be channeling you and Naor differently in the future?

Naor was doing what we will be doing in the near future, which is coming through with more force and experimenting with the best dialect to distinguish each of us clearly. At the ascended masters' retreat, Damiana was clearing her vessel, creating a clear and fluid channel through which we can communicate more clearly, as well as discovering another location that she can experience while we are coming by to make these sessions.

We continue seeing Damiana's progression going very well and moving forward quite rapidly. Be patient with it and you will receive the communication level that you seek. Don't underestimate these early sessions, however, for these are the base and skeleton of the structure you are creating, and nothing can come without it.

Do you perceive that Damiana's channel has improved as a result of the experience she had at the ascended masters' retreat? Are you experiencing her a little bit more clearly today?

Are *you* experiencing *me* more clearly today? (Smiles)

(Laughs) You're not supposed to answer a question with a question.

Yes, I do feel that the connection is stronger today.

I have a few more questions, if I may.

Indeed.

I want to talk about knowledge and wisdom. Books are important because they help us learn. However, most people forget most of what they read. What is a good way to acquire knowledge?

Through experience. This has always been an efficient way that we, the Pleiadians, have found to acquire knowledge. We are a very hands-on group. And while learning through a book helps share worlds that aren't always accessible to you, going out and truly *experiencing* all that your world has to offer can create a vast expansion of knowledge, perhaps not the kind your society has labeled and set for you, but a different type that is more inclusive and truly *known*, for you experienced it.

How is wisdom acquired?

Wisdom is acquired by listening to your instincts — paying attention to the voice inside your head that *has* experienced *All That Is*; that *has* experienced many past lives; that *has* experienced God.

If humans were able to use 100 percent of the brain, would we still be intellectually immature in comparison to the knowledge and wisdom contained in the universe?

Indeed you would. There are concepts that are beyond the human brain. However, don't underestimate how much of the brain you use, for it is actually a human myth that you only use a small percentage of your brain. Perhaps only a small percentage is used at a time, but all parts of your brain are used in different situations.

There are people on our planet who have brain damage. Yet, somehow through that damage another aspect of the brain has opened up. For example, some of these people may be socially undeveloped and yet they might have perfect memory recall. This indicates to me that we're *not* using 100 percent of our brain. If I can read a book and forget 90 percent of what I've read, there's clearly a great inefficiency in my use of the brain.

You're not using 100 percent of your brain at one time, but you do use all parts of it. That's why you have a memory that can be recalled through techniques. And you do have social skills. And you do have all the different parts that your brain represents. Regarding the many beings that do experience brain damage, paying attention and honoring their gifts and who they are on your planet is most important for the development of human consciousness and compassion.

What is memory? Where is memory actually stored?

Memory, while in physical form, is connected with your brain. It is part of your consciousness. This is why you can bring forth past life memories and out-of-body memories. Although these memories are often forgotten so that you can achieve this life's goals, that consciousness still exists and can be brought forth if needed. And every book you've ever read is still stored in that memory as well.

Where is memory stored? Is it stored in the brain? Is it stored in consciousness?

In consciousness within the brain in physical form. But you carry this consciousness with you after death and into future lives.

What is the best way to retain information? How can we improve our memory?

By finding out the best way in which you learn — visual, experiential, technical — and learning by these means. Realize that not everyone is the same and doesn't learn in the same way. There are many different ways to experience life.

Are the akashic records a type of memory?

In a way, a memory of the universe and *All That Is* — an all-inclusive library, so to speak.

Please explain how the akashic records are preserved.

They are preserved within the consciousness of the universe. Everything that you do, say, or think, everything that is, was, or will be, all resides within this universal, Godly consciousness that can be obtained, for the higher consciousness is connected with *All That Is*, creating this akashic record.

Thank you very much for coming through today. Once again, we feel honored to be having these communications with you. I do believe that today's connection is strong. Do you have anything else you'd like share with us before we end today's session?

Thank you. As always, the honor is all mine. Have a wonderful day. We'll speak again soon. In love and light. Many blessings.

We will not set forth rules for humanity, but when choosing what you think is best for your planet we suggest looking towards love, compassion, sharing, your brother, your sister, your planet Earth. Look towards positive growth, positive movement, and inclusive, all-together concepts that do not exclude individuals.

24

Greetings, it is I, Ilana. You are recreating yourself—redefining your physical existence — each and every day, so why not recreate on a grander scale? Do you not have faith in yourself as a creator to break down walls of yesterday and build a beautiful, brand new tomorrow? May I answer some questions?

This is difficult for many people because they're recreating their own unconscious patterns which are just reproducing the same results that they've gotten in the past. Can you speak about that?

You can become aware of these patterns, what is working in your life and what is not. Take time to pay attention and create the change you wish to see; bring it forth through your God-energy. Take time to discover and define what is appropriate and what is not. This is the best place to start so there aren't those unconscious choices from the past.

Many people are struggling with security issues, like how to make enough money to pay their bills and have food to eat. This conflicts with their wish to serve humanity, to do something constructive and important in life. How can people learn to resolve that apparent conflict?

This is something your society will have to come to terms with, finding an even balance for all beings so there isn't over-abundance and under-abundance, but equal security, safety, and food — a balance for all beings, taking care of and lifting up those who in the past have been left behind. And, perhaps giving up some securities that might seem nice and comforting but have no real value in your life other than as materialistic wants. They are no longer needed. Many beings need to come to terms with their relationship to the material world, building new relationships and connections with other beings.

Are you suggesting that it's important for starseeds to focus on their purpose and mission, building up their passion for that, rather than being so concerned about their own material comfort?

Indeed, for starseeds on their true path — lifting up others around them and bringing pure joy to themselves through their true passion — will be provided for in simple and dynamic ways.

How many starseeds are actually waking up to their true missions or working on them?

During this important time in Earth's history, many are awakening. Some are doing their mission without realizing it. Others could still use a nudge in the right direction. A good number of starseeds remain to be awakened, but many *are* awakening and becoming aware of their life purpose.

What is the best way to awaken these starseeds who remain asleep?

The connections will be made. The universe already has them in motion. So, your purposes and missions will come into focus. And those interactions — beings that need *your* assistance — will become clear and brought forth to you.

Are you saying that the universe and spiritual guides have already set into motion plans to awaken sleeping starseeds? Are you saying that some of these starseeds will be directed to Damiana to be sparked awake?

Indeed, that is exactly what I'm saying. And while many will awaken through these interactions, some may not, and you must not feel like you have failed in any way. They will awaken on their path when it is most appropriate. We can only make the connections and help guide as much as possible.

Adam was here the other day. He discussed densities and dimensions. I have a couple of follow-up questions. Can I ask you my questions?

Indeed, absolutely.

Are densities and dimensions merely concepts to help us become more loving and aware or do they actually exist in ways that can be scientifically observed and measured?

Both. Everything in the universe is conceptual in many ways and you create the reality in which you exist. However, these frequencies and vibrations that create different densities and dimensions can be measured, do exist, and your scientists will come to this conclusion at some point in your history.

I spoke to an astrophysicist. He said that energy and matter, or mass, are interchangeable, and because density is related to mass, energy also has density. Therefore, higher energy has *higher* density, not less density. Could you discuss this?

This is density in a different form. Higher frequency creates less density. Until you reach those higher frequencies, the density, while still existing around you, cannot be viewed or understood. There are mass and matter within densities of higher frequency, but until you are in a higher frequency, you cannot view it from your dimension.

Here on the Earth, our physicists understand that higher frequency is equated with higher energy, and since energy is interchangeable with mass, if you have higher energy you actually have *higher* mass or *higher* density. So, that's the confusion; our physicists equate higher energy with higher density, but in the terminologies that you and Adam provide higher energy is equated with dimensions that are *less* dense. How can angelic realms or spiritual worlds of higher frequency be *less* dense and *more* ethereal rather than the other way around?

Within your physical plane, the Earth plane, your scientists are making conclusions that work within *your* dimension and *your* density. Within *higher* frequencies and densities the dimensions and rules are somewhat different. While higher energy relates to higher density within Earth's physical plane in the third dimension in which you exist at this time, that is not necessarily so within the higher dimensions. Higher frequencies create these other dimensions; there is *less* density within them, which is different than the Earth plane.

Will this eventually be understood by our scientists?

As you move into higher dimensions with higher frequency, new discoveries and higher understanding will become clearer.

I have a couple of follow-up questions about extraterrestrials on the Earth. Adam said that several different extraterrestrial groups have communicated with our government and that some of these communications were through channeling but that others were through actual, physical interactions. How do extraterrestrials communicate with humans face-to-face? I assume they don't speak our language.

Many ETs are fluent in many different languages, including *all* of Earth's languages. While there are some ETs who are not fluent, the ones who have communicated with your government are fluent with Earth languages.

Does this mean that all of the ETs who have communicated with our government have biological apparatus allowing them to speak through vocal cords, like we have?

Most of them. There have been a few that have spoken face-to-face telepathically.

What is the Council of Intergalactic Relations?

The Council of Intergalactic Relations is a branch of the Extraterrestrial Council that was established by benevolent extraterrestrials in the galaxy who share a passion for moving forward to create a more dynamic and beautiful future for all who exist within the universe. We regulate and monitor interactions between different extraterrestrial races and watch over and protect many planets.

Who sits on the board of this council? Are there certain representatives from different extraterrestrial groups?

Indeed. We, the Pleiadians, the Alpha Centauri, the Sirians, the Essassani, the Orions, the LaZari... We also often have guests who interact from far distances of the universe. There are branches that exist in other parts of the universe as well.

What about the Ashtar Command? Who are they and where are they from?

The Ashtar Command has greatly assisted in moving humanity forward. They are extraterrestrial space brothers and sisters who exist mostly in a spaceship and not so much a home planet. They travel the many different reaches of the universe and are a joint consciousness of many different beings making up one unity. They, too, have a soft spot for humanity but lack understanding of human emotions and may become restless when emotions are involved.

Are they associated with the Council of Intergalactic Relations?

They, too, have a spot on our council.

How did shadow governments gain control over UFO technology and ET cover-ups?

Your government releases information to control humanity, sometimes as a fear tactic but also to cover up mass hysteria, for if humanity realized that your government was aware and letting extraterrestrials such as the Grays pick humans at will, there would be quite the uprising against them. And so, the "Men in Black" — as you've come to call them — have created a mass cover-up movement for technological reasons, for personal greed reasons, and also not to scare you too much — but just enough so that you won't go snooping for more information to find the truths within the universe. They keep you blissfully ignorant. The cover-up of extraterrestrials, such as ourselves who have made contact, is more for profit with big corporations on your planet. They don't necessarily want our assistance in finding alternative energy resources or cleaning up your atmosphere or stopping the production of what's destroying much of your planet, for many higher-ups on your planet are invested in these large corporations and aren't willing to risk that because they lack compassion on your planet.

Many people are concerned about a One World government. What is your opinion about this?

This, again, is something humanity will have to come to terms with. We think there is potential for an all-inclusive and "ruling by the heart" government that is focused on helping and taking care of the entire planet, bringing a balance between third world countries and multi-billionaire individuals. We do think a One World government has quite a lot of potential and we also understand the fear that humanity has in a government that does not share everyone's ideals. So if this were to come to be, you'd have to make sure the government truly has the peoples' needs in mind; not a corrupt government, as many are now.

Who or what is the Illuminati? Should we be afraid of secret groups trying to control the world?

Throughout humanity there have been many secret groups. Even Damiana's third eye travel the other day was to a very early Freemason gathering. [Damiana astral-traveled to a secret chamber beneath one of the pyramids in ancient Egypt where she witnessed Isis giving an inspiring talk to a group of early light workers. You can read about this in *Third Eye Awakening*.] Illuminati are a shadow government within themselves, and while such secrecy continues to exist on your planet, the needs of everyone will not be taken care of. Bringing forth honesty and trust — not having these secret societies any longer — and finding relatability within each other truly will help assist your society. Bringing everything onto the table to find out what you want and what you don't want for the future would be helpful.

I think of Freemasonry as a positive group trying to bring world peace and enlightenment to the planet. I always thought they were associated with the ascended masters and Spiritual Hierarchy. Although it's a secret

group, I understand that it has positive goals. I suppose that secrecy in any form is scary to a lot of people. Can you speak about that some more?

Indeed. A lot of that is true about Freemasonry. And while working for the good in any capacity is a positive thing, for trust and understanding to work on your planet, it's important to come forth and work in the light where everyone is aware of your energy and your work; this truly will benefit your planet. You cannot ask for one group to come forth and another to stay hidden, for this will create fear in many people.

What you're saying sounds similar to what Djwal Kuhl stated in some of the Alice Bailey teachings, where they talked about externalizing the Spiritual Hierarchy. For thousands of years the masters worked with light workers on the inner planes, but eventually their work and goals would need to be externalized. Is this related to what we're talking about?

Yes, indeed, that is exactly what we are speaking of — bringing forth all this work in *all* manners of secrecy, bringing it forth and externalizing it.

Are you suggesting that the masters are willing to become more well known and acknowledged as actually existing behind the scenes? Do you think it's important for more people to realize that channeling does exist and that some people are working with altruistic beings on the other side, such as ascended masters and benevolent extraterrestrials?

Yes, we would like to see that. However, not all of your world is ready for that at this time. So, showing discernment and caution is important, but not staying hidden or hiding your gift. Continue helping others to become aware of the reality of the universe.

Some of the information that you are revealing is quite controversial. For example, you said that our government is hiding important truths from us and using fear as a tactic of control. You said that some of the corporations harming our planet have reincarnated Reptilians at the helm. These are pretty outrageous claims. Damiana and I are the ones that will be going forward with these claims. How do you feel about that?

While in some ways Damiana is very meek, it is important that you are comfortable with the information that you put out there and are bold within yourselves realizing that there will be controversy with this path, with this mission. But we are with you *every* step of the way and will protect you.

We're 100 percent committed to this path; there's no question about that. My concern is whether some of these controversial claims can be confirmed. Where is the evidence that our government is withholding extraterrestrial information and that abductions are permitted in exchange for technology? This information will certainly stimulate deep emotions in people but how do we know that it's *true,* other than the fact that you're telling us that it is?

In this line of work, faith is necessary. As we go further down the line, there *will* be concepts and ideas that can't be proven on the Earth plane in your dimension at this time. And there *will* be controversy. There *will* be people who don't agree with it. However, if it is what *you* believe, if *you* trust the source, then it's important that you stand by these claims. There will be a time on your planet when these controversies will surface. ETs will make ourselves known within your very near future — within the next 5 to 15 years, as we see the energy unfolding. These concepts will become clear for the masses at some point.

Many people have strong feelings about population control. Do you think there is an ideal number of people to be living on our planet?

This is another challenge for humanity, for at this time there are many beings on your planet who are breeding without consequences. They are not taking care of and raising these children in the most appropriate way. For many souls, adoption is a positive way to go about raising children. You cannot tell someone not to breed, but you can provide more sex education, birth control, and help raise children on your planet in positive ways to continue the line in a more positive manner.

The Chinese government has limited the number of children families can have.

That is something you will all have to come to terms with. Whether that is something that you want for this country, other countries, or the whole world, is a challenge that humanity will have to face.

Do you think that our planet can handle eight or nine billion people if these children are raised consciously and families or countries are able to feed, clothe, and take care of them? Or do you think that's just too many people for our planet and we don't have enough resources to share with everyone?

I think you need to decide on that. As it is now, you're not feeding and clothing all the people that already exist on your planet. I think starting there is a good idea, before it gets to a point of so many more beings on your planet. It's important to feed and clothe the ones that already exist.

Well, that was another very enlightening session. I have many more questions. I don't think I will ever run out of questions, but I'll save them for later. Thank you for coming through. Do you have anything else you'd like to share with us before we end today's session?

Thank you. I do appreciate the time we spend together. In love and light. Many blessings.

We do not wish to interfere with your free will. We wish to empower humanity and aid your planet, help give you the confidence to go forth and create the civilization you wish to live in. Therefore, we will be extremely cautious regarding information we hand over to you. We will not give you all the answers, but we will help guide you in a reasonable direction.

25

Greetings my friends. It is I, Adam. May I answer some questions tonight?

Yes. Welcome, Adam. I'd like to start today's session with questions about international concerns. What is the best way to handle the global problem of hunger and people starving?

This is where a balance is much needed on your planet. There is overabundance, especially in this category, while others are starving, and this problem is all around you, not only in third world countries. Right here in your own community there are people starving. The problem can be addressed with a government that puts this as a priority — food, shelter, and healthcare as a minimum for *every* being on your planet. With that being said, assisting without interfering with personal karma is always a positive path to take in these situations of lower human experiences.

Does this mean lending money to other nations that have a high percentage of their population starving? Does this mean redistributing food or learning to produce more food? What exactly does this mean?

That is a challenge which humanity will have to face. However, you can come to a balance for humanity, giving up overabundance for a minimum, sharing and spreading. There are enough resources on your planet for natural growth to take place and provide for everyone. Others can be taught how to harvest and grow natural food. You can share with your brother and your sister.

Some people don't like this idea of redistributing wealth. They believe that it's better if the weak wither away and die, that somehow that's better for the human species.

Those particular beings are on their path of karma, but for your personal growth and gift to humanity, *you* can create that change. *You* have the power within you, and so do others who are awakening. You can shift the energy towards more positive growth on your planet towards helping and sharing with many different people.

A lot of nations don't have very fertile land in which to grow food, so they would need the help of outside nations. That brings up another question. Is there advanced technology to make it rain in the desert?

There are technologies to create different weather patterns. However, a balance of these climates is actually important to your planet. There's a strain on all your climates at this time because of the depletion of your atmosphere and desecration of much of the natural growth on your planet. You can learn to work with the Earth's natural growth in different areas. Your planet has become much more global within the last several years and you are able to equally distribute from other more fertile grounds.

Do you think there's any benefit to seeding the atmosphere in arid regions to produce rain or would this have a negative influence on the environment? Do you think this is moving in the wrong direction, not really addressing the root of the problem such as global warming?

Indeed. It is a quick fix and not a remedy. Also, it can create a different effect than what you are expecting, for there is an abundance of rain on some parts of your planet and dry heat on others. Start at the base, the root of the problem. Come up with new energy sources. Look to your Sun. Look to the Earth's plates. Stop the drilling. Teach about the importance of the planet. Shed old ways of the past, starting anew.

Please discuss changes that are occurring in the Middle East. Several countries such as Egypt, Libya, and Syria are experiencing revolutions. The people seem to be leaning toward democracy.

Yes, this is a very exciting time for those countries, for much of Earth's last 2,000 years have been small revolutions that have created and opened up new opportunities for those individuals. There is potential for democracy to begin in those countries; that is where we see the energy heading.

Some people wonder whether some nations are ready for democracy. Is that a possibility?

Anything is a possibility. Possibilities are endless. However, democracy in its basic form has quite a lot of potential and we see, if they choose to head in that direction, quite an abundance of growth and change that they are overly ready for.

A few years ago, Palestinians were encouraged to have open elections and they voted in Hamas, which many nations consider a terrorist organization. Some people don't believe that the election was in the best interests of the Palestinians even though it occurred through a democratic process. Can you talk about that?

Indeed. This is one of the problems with politics. While it seemed like a democratic process on the surface — much like America's current "democratic" elections — there are people working under the surface to sway these elections in certain ways, and this power is still very much present in Palestine.

Why do cultures develop customs that cause harm? For example, some societies have promoted animal and human sacrifices, or footbinding. Even today, some cultures practice female genital mutilation.

All of this is karmic in nature. These are customs that have to do with basic human instincts and human nature, for out of the physical body such ideas and concepts do not exist. Through time, humanity has stuck to old customs and religious ideas that bring them closer to their God figure or closer to each other in many ways. And while you look at some of these concepts as very taboo, like female genitalia mutilation, in your country every day there is male genitalia mutilation that goes unnoticed and seems perfectly normal.

Are you talking about circumcision?

Indeed. Humanity will have to decide whether to continue some of these traditions or whether to throw out these old ideas for something higher and newer.

Our nation promotes capitalism where businesses compete against each other to produce the best products and make the most money. What are the advantages and disadvantages of this system?

Capitalism can create a thriving economy. However, it also creates monopolies, throwing mom-and-pop and individual companies under the bus. Creating a balance where individual companies can thrive without so much corruption, where these larger companies are taking over and creating monopolies, is in your economy's best interest — finding a mutual agreement between your brothers and sisters.

Without competition, monopolies do occur. Is there an alternative?

Again, it's important to find that balance where there is natural competition, not corporate competition with greedy businessmen blackmailing and backstabbing. It can be healthy where both thrive, growing side-by-side without stepping on other people's toes.

I have a few questions about the United States Constitution. Do you think this is one of the more enlightened documents on the planet?

I think it has a lot of positive ideas that are no longer put into action. Perhaps it's time for a rewriting of the Constitution for a new time.

Does the U.S. Constitution cover most of the important principles?

We don't think it covers *all* of the important principles. More energy can be put into love, compassion, the environment, and raising your children in a positive way. It's a modern world that you're living in, and creating a more enlightened Constitution with modern concepts — not throwing out the Constitution, but refreshing it for a more global use — would be a good idea.

Who would sit on the committee to create a new Constitution and how would they agree on its contents? That would be a difficult task.

Indeed, but by finding those individuals from different sectors with lots of different ideas to bring to the table — new, outside-the-box ideas — and listening to many beings, and always coming from a place of love, it's hard to go wrong.

A lot of politicians have very simple ideas about what should go into the Constitution. Some have proposed frivolous amendments such as outlawing gay rights or coercing Americans to respect the American flag.

When you come from a place of love, you can't go wrong — love for every single being on your planet and respect for different ways of life. Not rules to segregate, but rules to include.

Do you think it would be a good idea to create a Constitution of the World?

That is something you have to come to terms with, but where you are at with a globalized society, we think this would be a positive look towards the future.

Can you provide a few ideas about what you would include in a Constitution of the World?

We will not set forth rules for humanity, but when choosing what you think is best for your planet we suggest looking towards love, compassion, sharing, your brother, your sister, your planet Earth. Look towards positive growth, positive movement, and inclusive, all-together concepts that do not exclude individuals.

Some differences aren't about exclusion. For example, many people believe in spanking: "spare the rod, spoil the child." So there would be arguments about how to raise or discipline our children. It would be very difficult to agree and codify that into some kind of a Constitution.

Indeed, and that is something humanity is going to have to face. However, finding that power within yourselves to move forward, to look outside the box, and to stand up for what you believe in has its rewards.

The other day you gave a good summary of some extraterrestrial groups that have visited the Earth. Please discuss any ET groups from Orion. Is Naor of LaZarus associated with any of the Orion groups?

There are three main groups that reside within your constellation of Orion: the LaZari, the Orions, and the Scion. All three of them reside in different dimensions but are actually quite similar in nature. Naor will tell you more about his home planet and their journey when he feels the timing is right, so I will leave that to him.

Ilana implied that secrecy breeds fear and that it would be better for the planet if secret groups were open and honest about their plans. Is secrecy ever beneficial and necessary?

For the protection of oneself in mind; for that purpose we can understand secrecy. However, as your planet moves forward and globalizes, bringing forth these secret societies that are creating much fear, releasing that fear to raise a global vibration, would help move your planet in the right direction.

Do you think that I'm missing any important questions? Are there any topics that *you* think I should be asking about or that *you* think it's important for us to know about?

The flow of our sessions is going in a very positive direction and many topics are being covered. We will continue planting concepts in your head throughout the days ahead and the sessions will continue their natural flow.

Well, that's interesting because my next question is related to what you just said. Where does inspiration come from?

The higher consciousness that is One with *All That Is* — that is you, that is me, and that is God. Inspiration can spark from this universal consciousness.

Is this the same place where ideas for new inventions come from?

Yes. Most often it's this higher Self, higher consciousness, and it's often why many ideas repeat themselves in patterns throughout history.

What do you mean?

When you have an idea, for example, and don't execute it and then years later someone else comes up with that idea, it's from this universal consciousness.

There are many examples where we go through history without a certain idea or invention and then suddenly two or three people in different parts of the world are all vigorously working towards the same idea or racing to be the first to create the same invention. Are they tapping into this universal well of consciousness or do enlightened extraterrestrials seed humanity with these new ideas and technology?

Can't it be both?

Are you saying that people can be internally inspired to reach out to higher consciousness and manifest innovative ideas while extraterrestrials and spiritual beings simultaneously filter these concepts down to them?

Their idea, their consciousness, is connected with ours, so it can be both. We can spread concepts and ideas or their higher consciousness can connect with *All That Is*, with others vigorously working on the same idea. Everyone is connected.

How exactly do you inspire people with ideas? I assume that people can resist those ideas. What if I am not paying attention? Can you override my lack of attention or do I have to be in tune? How does that work?

We can send you an idea but it is up to you to execute it, whether you are paying attention or not. That is where our energy ends and yours begins.

Do all people have multiple alliances with different soul groups? Are religious, cultural and national affiliations really deeper links to a family of souls with common ideas and purposes?

You are *all* connected, and the many "I AMs" that make up who you are, are connected. Your gender, age group, religion, culture, community; all of these are groups that you are linked to in a karmic, soul family way.

Do accidents ever truly occur?

That is an idea, a concept, that you will have to decide.

Do coincidences ever occur?

Again, that is for your choices on this planet. However, everything is linked and planned out ahead of time.

So is anything ever truly random?

You do have free will on your planet, and while you do have a higher plan, there is an even balance between the choices that you make and a set goal. You see this in astrology daily.

Where did Edgar Cayce get his information? Was he channeling another being?

He was channeling his higher Self and higher consciousness of *All That Is*.

Thank you, Adam, for coming through once again. I look forward to your inspiration and having more of these wonderful sessions.

Everything is unfolding at the proper rate. We are eager and excited for all the energy and time you have put into spreading these words of love and light. We will continue again soon. Many blessings. In love and light.

26

Good morning. It is I, Adam. We are almost wrapping up our project. Naor and I have enjoyed working with you day after day, but there are many extraterrestrials and beings of Light who would like to have their say. After this project ends and others begin, it will be up to you whether you want to continue with us in the future or bring through many other beings. That being said, I'd like to start off today by giving you a little of our history as the Pleiadians.

During Atlantean times there was a clear-cut line between those dedicated to God, their brothers, sisters, and the Law of One, and those who denied it and focused on greed, ego, and selfish acts. This is being repeated in Earth history today. During that time in Atlantis, we, the Pleiadians, walked among Earthlings and were very close with them, but this clear-cut line developed between us as well. Many Pleiadians chose a lack of faith in themselves and God. They helped the humans who weren't spiritual in nature develop clones, mutants, and technology that they weren't yet ready for. There was a cosmic battle among Pleiadians during the same time as the flood of Atlantis. Those Pleiadians have set up in your constellation, your area, of Andromeda. They are never far from our hearts but choose a different way of life. Understanding past incidents and your history is important so as not to make the same mistakes, helping to bring those with different values up to higher consciousness, including *all* instead of creating two different worlds. May I answer some questions today?

Were the Pleiadians reincarnated on Atlantis as humans or did they come down from the heavens as extraterrestrials and walk among the humans as a separate species?

During Atlantean times many extraterrestrial species were welcomed in their natural form on your planet by the humans. Yes, the Pleiadians were Pleiadian beings at the time.

According to Plato, the last Atlantean flood was about 12,000 years ago. That doesn't seem too long ago for there to have been a division between Pleiadians.

Time for us is a very different matter, so we only have events in our history.

What does that mean?

This concept of time exists for humans. The Sun comes up, the Sun goes down. You've created these time limitations on your planet. For us, we don't have those limitations and so there is no difference to us between 50,000 days in the past or 50,000 days in the future — only significant events that have happened here and now. I realize that it's very confusing when there *is* time in your understanding.

It's a little disappointing to learn that Pleiadians, who are spiritually advanced, had conflicts among each other not too long ago. Now it seems clear that even if humans advance spiritually, at any point in time we could revert back to our lesser ways.

That is true and is something you will always have to be aware of in your spiritual advances, always keeping yourself at a raised vibration, not letting yourself fall down. You must realize that we were not always as spiritually advanced or understanding as we are at this time. We had developed much like humanity in many ways. You must not look at this event with a lack of faith in us. Instead, realize the growth that *you* can achieve from conflicts such as these and by choosing different ways than the past.

Once again, it's discouraging to realize that Pleiadians are thousands of years ahead of humans, yet some members of your group reverted to selfish acts and less spiritual inclinations.

I apologize if this was too soon to bring up these concepts. We, the Pleiadians who come through and speak with you every day, are not the same ones who separated and went backwards during Atlantean times. We have always stuck to the Law of One.

Please don't ever apologize for sharing the truth with us. Were there any signs that some of the Pleiadians were not abiding by the highest principles before they emigrated to Atlantis?

We have grown the same way that humanity is growing — through technological advancements, spiritual advancements, and by trying to make our civilization the purest, most loving, most advanced, all-inclusive civilization possible. Over time, we have reached that point. However, we were quite divided with all different types of beings on Pleiades throughout our culture with different concepts and ideas. And during our time on Atlantis with humanity, many of these differences became abundantly clear.

Are the breakaway Pleiadians who now reside in the constellation of Andromeda seventh-dimensional beings? What are their goals and purposes at this time?

They are fourth-dimensional beings and are quite similar to the Earth with their goals and concepts. Many of them have forgotten their history with us, with you, with any of the universe, and they are very stuck in their world. Their technology is somewhat more advanced than yours, but they have problems very similar to those on the planet Earth. However, there are light workers on their planet as well.

Thank you for sharing that. I have some health-related questions. Health authorities strongly promote vaccines as a way to stop the spread of disease. In the United States they recommend that infants receive eight different vaccines at two months of age, then again at four and six months of age. What are your thoughts about this?

Some developments on your planet are moving backwards, not forwards; exposing young children to the diseases that reside in the vaccines is causing harm on your planet. Money and corporate corruption has become more important to many beings than true development towards destroying disease on your planet. Proper development has been thrown away.

What do you mean by that? What is proper development?

There are herbal and natural remedies for all the diseases on your planet. God left you with all the necessary tools for self-healing; vaccinations have become destructive.

Health authorities say that vaccines save millions of lives every year. For example, they claim that by vaccinating people against polio, which can cause paralysis and even death, the disease has been eliminated from most of the world. Please speak about that.

Polio was already becoming a disease of the past. However, the polio vaccine was one of the only vaccines with the correct intention; once monetary gain was discovered in the vaccine industry, this became more of the focus rather than actually helping the planet. More time should be spent by individuals doing proper research, finding what's best for them and their family instead of just going along with the herd because a so-called expert told them what to do. The resources are there for each and everyone to discover what's best for themselves.

It's interesting that you mentioned the term "herd" and that people should not necessarily go along with the herd. Health authorities claim that *everyone* has to be vaccinated to provide "herd immunity" to the group. They claim that if some people refuse vaccines then the entire group will be threatened with disease. What are your thoughts on this?

This is for monetary gain on their part, for humans have been on your planet for thousands of years taking care of themselves. You're born into the world with natural immunities that aren't going to cause harm to anyone else. And so, it's just manipulation on their part.

Health authorities say that if unvaccinated children catch a disease, they can spread it to other people. They also say that some people have weak immune systems and they're not able to be vaccinated. Therefore, if people who *can* be vaccinated don't get vaccinated, they threaten these other people with disease, the ones who have the weak immune systems. What do you have to say about that?

Again, this is manipulation tactics on their part. It does not work like that. There are natural immunities that you're born with and there are natural remedies for those illnesses. The vaccines are causing much more harm than good.

If children are not vaccinated, they're not allowed in school unless their parents sign a waiver. Many employers are now requiring their workers to receive vaccines or they will lose their jobs. Do you think these are good policies?

These are all concepts and ideas that will need to be put on the table for a new world, to decide what is best for that new civilization, throwing away old concepts and ideas, doing proper research for what *is* appropriate in your new world, and coming to new conclusions.

Health authorities proclaim that vaccines are safe but children seem to be sicker than they've ever been. For example, more children than ever before have attention deficit problems, food allergies, asthma, and autism. Are these conditions related to vaccines?

Absolutely. These are all products of vaccine damage.

I have a few health-related questions that I may have asked before, but I'd like to get more information on them. Do germs cause disease?

They do not cause it, but they can influence it. If you weaken your immune system, often through emotional trauma, stress, or an argument, these all put strain on your body and lower your immune system. It makes you susceptible to certain germs that are out there, but there are always natural cures for these diseases.

What is the best way to avoid catching a contagious disease?

Keeping your vibration as high as possible. Not letting anger, doubt or fear in, but staying happy and loving, relaxing when you are stressed, stepping out of a fight and just listening, so as not to lower your immune system.

Are diseases truly contagious or is it possible to expose oneself to disease and be strong enough not to catch it?

Absolutely. By keeping your vibrations in a positive, higher frequency, you can step into any situation — including highly contagious diseases — and not let it affect you.

Is it possible to go through life without disease or is getting sick part of the human experience?

It's part of the human experience in the third dimension. However, these diseases will become a thing of the past as you continue raising your vibration into higher dimensions.

Do we want to avoid disease or does sickness serve a positive function?

There are karmic reasons why some individuals have disease in their life, but individuals, especially those on a spiritual path, want to keep their vibration high and their vessel clean for the light work.

What is the best way to deal with epidemics of disease?

Be aware of the epidemic, do research on it, keep your vibration high, and discover your own best plan of protection.

Here on the Earth, scientists experiment on animals to discover cures to human diseases. Do you think this is necessary?

This is a very touchy subject for humans. We do not think it is appropriate to be testing on animals. Finding a proper way to discover new cures, perhaps testing on human volunteers, is more appropriate, although that is rather touchy as well.

Do you have diseases on Pleiades?

We resonate to a higher frequency. We have eliminated disease on our planet.

If diseases are necessary for the balance of karma, why are we allowed to find cures for some of them? People still need to balance their karma.

It is all part of that plan, that karma. Some diseases do not have cures yet and some individuals have chosen that karma. As you move forward into higher consciousness — getting on a path of dharma over karma — disease will become a thing of the past.

Do diseases and physical ailments correspond with mental and emotional attitudes? For example, is cancer related to a personality type? Are ailments of the eye related to an inability to see something clearly?

In some situations, yes. When you say something mean to someone and you get a sore throat, this is very much a karmic situation. Being aware and paying attention, recognizing those connections, will help you come out clean on the other side.

If we have a problem in the body somewhere, is this always a clue to a weakness within our mind or how we are relating to other people?

Very often it is, so looking at that and trying to find that connection will help you cure it.

Recently, a UFO was seen hovering over the Temple Mount, or Dome of the Rock, a religious site in Israel that is considered holy to Christians, Muslims, and Jews. Although the UFO was filmed by a few different people, there is controversy over whether this was a real UFO or an elaborate hoax. Would you comment on this?

This was a real UFO. It belonged to the Sirians. Many extraterrestrials are testing the water, so to speak, of humanity, making themselves more known, for within the next several years (as we feel the energy going), we hope to reconnect with humanity in physical form.

So, this UFO was an actual spaceship that belonged to the Sirian group of extraterrestrials?

Absolutely.

What message were they trying to convey?

They were just gauging humanity's reaction, for they and many of the other extraterrestrials have been letting themselves get "caught" on film and by the human eye just to feel the energy of the planet and measure how concepts and energy are changing over time.

This UFO was filmed by three or four different individuals from different angles. Some of the videos seem to be honest while others seem to be part of an elaborate hoax trying to cover up the truth. Could you speak about that?

Yes. This is quite often the case when there are UFO sightings on your planet. There will be some videos that are real and then many of your governments will put out fake ones to trick humanity into thinking they are *all* fake. Yes, some of them were fake and some were real. However, there were many more individuals who viewed that UFO without filming it.

A massive earthquake in Japan caused nuclear reactors to leak radioactive material into the atmosphere. How much radioactivity is spreading around the world and how dangerous is it?

This radioactivity is in your atmosphere and you are, unfortunately, breathing it in every day. This is a result of what humans have created over time. You can help protect yourself against this activity through natural remedies; many green plants and mushrooms will help build up your immune system against it.

This event took place six months ago and yet they still don't seem to have it under control. Do you see them making any progress?

Progress is being made inch by inch at a very slow rate and it will eventually be contained. However, the damage is already done and has contaminated your atmosphere, and nuclear radiation from the past is still contaminating your air today.

What do you mean?

The bombs dropped in Japan, the release of atomic energy in Chernobyl; these are all still contaminating modern-day air on your planet.

Should we be concerned about other nuclear reactors?

Yes and no. You shouldn't live your life worrying about whether there's going to be nuclear warfare or that your planet will be destroyed. However, it is in humanity's best interest to make conscious choices to clean up the atmosphere, head towards more natural resources, and find solutions to eliminate nuclear and atomic power.

How concerned should we be about terrorists gaining access to radioactive material and creating a nuclear weapon or bomb?

You should not let this interfere with your everyday activities, for fear and doubt are low forms of vibration. You want to always resonate at high frequencies. That is a concern of your planet; finding ways to eliminate nuclear and choosing other resources is in your best interest.

What is the likelihood of this actually occurring? Do you think that our security measures are adequate to protect against this possibility?

It is a possibility. There is always a chance for any situation to take place.

Damiana and I are open and receptive to whatever you and the ascended masters consider most appropriate for her development and purpose. Do you have any comments about this?

Indeed. We would like to continue with future projects. However, we will also let more extraterrestrials come forth with their energy and their messages of light, for this is at its very beginning stages, and we are just helping Damiana redevelop her gift. We see it going great places.

It seems too early to publish this material. Copies of my book, *Gadzooks: Extraterrestrial Guide to Love, Wisdom and Happiness* are still available. What do you have to say about that?

We agree that it isn't quite time to publish this book, for we will create the right structure. It will become clear when it's appropriate, and *Gadzooks* will have its day in the limelight as well.

Can we look forward to additional sessions with you?

Indeed. I will continue coming forth even after the book is done, for we do see future books as well.

But we do have more material for this book, do we not?

We do.

Thank you for coming through once again. Do you have anything else you'd like to share with us before we end today's session?

Many blessings. In love and light.

27

It is time to heal your Earth, starting from the tiny seed and roots, all the way up to the strongest oak tree. Take time to nurture her so that she can grow and share her love with the planet. Sharing and healing your Mother Earth can bring unity upon your planet, for this is something all humans have in common. You are all of the Earth and can heal yourselves through understanding and unity. This silly idea of being alone in the universe is part of human instinct, thinking you were alone in your individual countries, and then a new understanding was found. You have become much more global in nature. The next step, naturally, is into the cosmos.

My name is PollyAnn. I am part of the Arcturian Galactic Federation. We are a foundation of love and light, sending our energy throughout the universe. May I answer some questions?

Yes, welcome. We've been working mostly with Pleiadians and a few other groups. What else can you share with us about Arcturians?

There are many extraterrestrial groups and Light beings who have so much to share with your planet. We eagerly await the right moment to make our presence known through Damiana. Arcturians are ethereal in body and vibrate at a seventh-dimensional frequency. We radiate love and light, constantly sending this energy back and forth to all galaxies and corners of the universe. We feel that it is our life's work to assist planets that are falling back, in some regards, to help bring them forth and help heal energy that has weakened over time. As Earth ascends universally into a higher dimension, where it once was, we are overseeing it and helping you help your planet in the most efficient way.

What exactly is the Arcturian Federation? Who belongs to it and what is the mission?

The mission is to spread love and light. We open up the federation to all who wish to join. It is mostly made up of Arcturians, however the Ashtar Command, Pleiadians, Sirians, and certain extraterrestrial individuals have put their names on the council as well.

How long have you been working with humanity?

We have been working with humanity since the time of Lemuria, then on and off throughout your history.

Have you ever had a physical presence on the Earth?

We are not physical in nature, but, yes, our ethereal energy has been physicalized during Atlantean and Lemurian times.

What is the history of human beings? Did they evolve from apes?

It is a combination between your theory of Darwinism and Creationism. There is a link between humanity and apes going all the way back to microorganisms. The soul has had its own journey as well in a very similar manner.

Where did human civilization begin on the planet?

There was a time when your continents were much more connected, although pieces, like Atlantis, have fallen out. So, humanity was able to spread out across these continents that were all one at the time. However, much of your modern-day civilization originated from parts of Africa.

I also read that it may have started near Mesopotamia or near where Iraq is today, near the Tigress and Euphrates rivers. Did early civilizations begin there as well?

Indeed. There were early civilizations throughout the whole Middle East and African area that then spread out further. Then the continents spread out making it seem as if civilizations also began in Australia and South America, but it was originally all one continent.

There are different races of humanity on the Earth: White, Black, Indian and Asian. How did the different races evolve or get started?

This is part of the growth for humanity. A xenophobic outlook that has been with much of humanity over time still exists and will become clear when extraterrestrial life makes its presence much more known. Different races (colors) on your planet adapted very much to the area on the globe in which they lived. Many of the races closer to the equator and to the Sun have adapted higher doses of melatonin in their skin for protection. It wasn't necessary for ones further away. Realize that you are all human; no one is lesser or greater. Embrace each other and the many beautiful colors on your planet, spreading that to meetings with extraterrestrials in the future.

Is there any evidence on the Earth of extraterrestrial visitations?

We think so. The crop circles and pyramids received extra-terrestrial help. Easter Island, Stonehenge, and many of the crashes that have happened. Governments have covered them up, but there are individual sightings of UFOs.

Did extraterrestrials ever die on the Earth when they visited Atlantis? Were their bodies buried? Will their bones ever be discovered?

Not during Atlantean times. However, there have been accidents by present-day extraterrestrials who have made visits, and those bones can be discovered. Other extraterrestrial bones and bodies have been discovered although governments have covered this up. There are also extraterrestrial bodies that haven't yet decomposed.

Is this because the government is keeping them on ice?

Indeed, and they have done much research on them.

Do extraterrestrials ever visit the other planets in our solar system?

Absolutely. There is traveling and visitation through all of your planets and on many of the other planets throughout the universe as well. Civilizations exist on your planets in higher dimensions.

Did extraterrestrials ever leave physical evidence of their existence on any of the planets in our solar system?

When you reach these higher dimensions, new discoveries on many of these planets will be made by your scientists, but not until you reach these higher dimensions.

Is there any special significance to our planet's Moon other than as a satellite of the Earth?

Your Moon also has life upon it in higher dimensions, and it represents many of the connections that you have with *All That Is,* helping influence menstrual cycles in women and tides on your planet. It is also linked to the electromagnetic energy within your planet.

You said that in higher dimensions other civilizations exist on our Earth's moon and on other planets in our solar system, yet they seem quite barren to us. What are they like in these higher dimensions? Are they barren in those dimensions as well?

Not so much. There is much activity going on in the higher dimensions, whole civilizations and life, large populations of extraterrestrial groups living on these planets. It only looks barren from your point of view in your dimension.

That is confusing. Damiana visited Pleiades with her third eye and saw a lot of plant life and a very natural planet. Yet, it's apparently not a physical planet because it's in the seventh dimension. So it's very confusing to look at the Moon, see that it's dusty and barren, yet hear you say that it's teeming with life.

Damiana, during her third eye travels, can go into these higher dimensions and experience them. She can go to the Moon and see life that exists there, if she so chooses.

Are there multi-layered civilizations on some planets? For example, is it possible for there to be one civilization on Neptune in the fourth dimension and another civilization on Neptune in the fifth dimension, and so forth?

That is possible. That's something to think about Earth as well. Others are living among you in higher dimensions.

Yes, Adam told us that elementals live on the Earth in the fourth dimension.

Indeed, this is true. We work very closely with them to help try and keep balance on your planet.

Where do the Grays live when they are on the Earth?

Grays don't live on your planet. They often visit your atmosphere with their spaceships, but it is only by accident if they crash upon your planet, which your government will often cover up quite quickly. The Grays are mostly nomadic in nature and don't really reside on a planet any longer. However, they do have mother ships, so to speak.

If the Grays are so technologically advanced, how is it possible that they end up crashing on the Earth?

It is rare, but mistakes have been made due to confusion within your atmosphere, going too close to the Earth's magnetic rays and creating a whirlpool of magnetic energy that pulls them in. This is very rare, however.

I thought that some of the Grays are on the Earth, alive and in communication with some of our secret government officials.

This is true. There are Grays who reside within your U.S., Russian, and Korean governments. There are some who were captured and work with your government. There are others who visit, do trades, and communicate with your government, but they do not live here, per se.

When the Grays are here, does our government provide food and shelter for them?

They do not stay for a very long time. When some are captured, the Grays will make trades with the government to get them back. The others are taken care of.

Who pays for the government's hidden extraterrestrial agenda? Where do they get the money?

The funds come from many of the large corporations on your planet. Fragments of your tax dollars go towards it as well.

Is this a hidden budget, because I haven't seen any official documents showing that my tax dollars are going to the extraterrestrial agenda?

It is very much a hidden budget disguised in other agendas.

How many different extraterrestrial species are currently residing on the Earth or within the Earth's atmosphere?

You are visited daily by several dozen different extra-terrestrials. The Pleiadians monitor and make sure that there is always proper intent when visiting. The Pleiadians reside right outside your atmosphere making sure that those who visit will not harm you.

What are some of the technologies that were given to humans by extraterrestrials?

Some of the fuel-efficient cars contain technology from extraterrestrials, and the internet. You use "out of this world" technologies everyday: GPS systems, smartphones, plus laser and fiber optics for noninvasive surgeries. Most of the more modern space exploration done by NASA and other leading country's scientists was donated from extraterrestrials. Even electricity in its modern form was originally discovered by Nikola Tesla, who was connected to the space brothers in his own way. There is also much technology that has not been shown to the public yet that was given by extraterrestrials, such as hovercrafts, spaceships, and different resources, including more natural resources energy. We hope your government will realize the true value that some of these technologies have when shared with the masses.

Why would extraterrestrials give the government information about natural resources energy when they know that it might not end up in the hands of the masses?

The Pleiadians have faith in many beings. Once the communication was there, they hoped your governments would take these resources and this knowledge to better your planet. Seeing as that is not necessarily being done, they've chosen to work with individuals, such as yourselves, to help get the message out about alternative energy sources.

Damiana and I have not received any specific information about how to utilize the Earth's magnetic fields or develop natural resources.

You will receive that kind of information when it's most appropriate and when the communication is clearer. That kind of information is very important to the Pleiadians and they don't want to risk any sort of confusion.

You make it sound like the Pleiadians were overly trusting or even gullible in giving important information to governments.

The Pleiadians are well aware of everything that your government does and doesn't do. They knew this when they shared these alternative resources with them. The Pleiadians are highly intelligent and also very understanding and non-judgmental, even towards shifty governments.

How much information can extraterrestrials give to humans before it is considered interfering with our own affairs or growth?

This is something that we have to be very cautious about, for we do not wish to interfere with your free will. We wish to empower humanity and aid your planet, help give you the confidence to go forth and create the civilization you wish to live in. Therefore, we will be extremely cautious regarding information we hand over to you. We will not give you all the answers, but we will help guide you in a reasonable direction.

I have a question about the channeling process. Is there a difference between channeling and receiving information telepathically?

Only definitions that Earth has given it. But, no, they are basically the same.

Some channeled information seems to arrive as thought bubbles that need to be interpreted into words. Other channelings seem to arrive in precise language. Can you elaborate on these apparent differences?

This is all about the level of communication, how tuned in the individual is. The thought bubbles are often a very basic way of transmitting information. While the direct communication can often be confused for the individual's own thoughts, it is more of a shared communication between the channeler and the being that is being channeled.

Is there any meaning to something that "exists across the veil" or is this just another way to describe non-physical worlds?

This is metaphor for humanity's understanding of life before birth and after death.

Alice Bailey received a lot of very specific esoteric information from the ascended master Djwal Kuhl. Did she receive it through a normal channeling process?

Yes, she was very tuned in and the telepathic communication between the two of them was extremely clear. Damiana can reach that level of clarity with time.

Are the Alice Bailey teachings still valid today? Is the information meant for anyone in particular?

Oh, absolutely. The Alice Bailey teachings are some of the clearest channeled information upon your planet and they are very pertinent, especially for today's energy. They are meant for those who seek it out, as is all channeled information. Those who seek the highest truths, who want more answers, can find the information. It is available to those who look for it.

Where is Alice Bailey today?

Alice Bailey ascended. She is working on the other side of the veil trying to help influence certain channels, pushing humanity forward towards a better future.

Is there anything the extraterrestrials can do to help Damiana clear her channel or is this something that she has to do on her own?

We help very often during meditations, working on proper frequency and energy, but this will develop over time in the most appropriate way as Damiana continues getting used to the channeling process and redeveloping her gift.

Sometimes Damiana feels like she's ready to have an extraterrestrial come through her, more like trance channeling, and yet that does not seem to be developing.

It is, with baby steps. It will happen over time. It's something we can't rush, for timing in this process is extremely important, and when that is most appropriate, it will happen.

What else would you like to share with us while you have this opportunity? Will we be hearing from you again in the future?

You will hear from me again. I wanted to come through and make my presence known. We will be working together in the future, as will many extraterrestrials who want to have their say and their presence made known upon your planet. I send to you many blessings. In love and light.

Feel the love that flows through you; it is higher existence operating. In everyday activities find love for every being, everyone you come in touch with — your best friend and your greatest enemy.

28

Greetings. It is I, Adam. May I answer some questions today?

Yes, hi Adam. It's been awhile since we last spoke. Welcome back.

Thank you. I've been working silently, adjusting Damiana for future sessions.

Please talk about the Spiritual Hierarchy. Is this the same group as the Brotherhood of Light?

Indeed. There are many names — mostly for humanity's understanding — for the many groups working for the greater good of humanity from the other side. Many are a part of this Hierarchy or Great White Brotherhood, including the ascended masters, benevolent extraterrestrials (such as ourselves), the archangels, angels, and many souls such as starseeds, working from the other side. They have been around since the beginning of time helping humanity evolve and reach a better place of higher enlightenment.

Do some of them incarnate onto the Earth? Are some of them actually here walking on the Earth?

Indeed, some of them are here in this room.

Please talk about the rays. Are these a type of cosmic energy?

Indeed. Color is a form of vibration and these different rays are different forms of vibration. Different beings associate better with different rays that also connect with the energy balls that you call chakras. The seven rays are related to the seven colors of the rainbow; each brings in different energy — all positive and enlightening.

I read that there are rays of science and rays of art, that type of idea. Could you speak about that?

Indeed. There are rays that combine with different areas of humanity, such as science, philosophy and art. These correlate with vibrations, creating layers to the human experience.

Is the number of people who are identifying with and expressing the functions of each individual ray evenly distributed among humanity?

Perhaps it was diverse when souls first entered the Earth plane, however at this time on your planet it is not balanced between these different rays, these different groups. There are many beings that have lost association or relatability with these different rays or they focus on a certain subject for monetary gain only. Focusing on these different rays and your own inspiration and inclinations would help create a balance on your planet. Allowing yourself to be drawn to art, music, science, or other natural inclinations, and continuing with the energy that you feel, would create a more balanced planet.

What is art? Is art associated with beauty?

Art is associated with beauty in that it is different for each individual. However, art does not necessarily have to be "beautiful." There are many different ways to express and combine inspiration and intent into a creative force that is physicalized.

Please talk about the different types of self-delusion or ways in which people deceive themselves into believing things that are not true.

Fear is a common form of manipulation on your planet. Through fear many beings create false comforts or religion or beliefs. Out of this fear they create these illusions for themselves. Raising your vibration to exclude this fear that controls many beings on your planet will permit clearer truths to come into view.

Is fear the only way that people allow themselves to become deluded?

Fear is the central concept that other, smaller delusions can spin off of. There are many smaller fears, like not fitting in or not getting along with others or not doing research for oneself. These seem scary to some people. Believing what your parents taught you without questioning it, or believing a certain belief simply because it sounds plausible or comforting, often creates these illusions as well.

In the Alice Bailey teachings, Djwal Kuhl talks about glamours — types of maya or self-delusions — where light workers curb their full potential.

Glamour is often related to the human ego. It is an illusion that not many humans even recognize. Releasing your glamour, shedding that cloak, showing a little humility, will serve you well. Do not get wrapped up in the many illusions that come with the early stages on a path of enlightenment.

Yes, many people allow their egos to take over without realizing it. For example, I have observed that some light workers place too much emphasis on believing they have a very special path or purpose. How can we avoid getting caught up in such glamours when they so easily influence our behaviors without our conscious awareness?

Develop true self-awareness. Recognize these glamours, seeing them for what they are. Be conscious of all the energy that you encounter as you head down a path of enlightenment. Release the energies you don't wish to keep. Be encouraged and confident, but realize that *anyone* can choose this path and everyone *will* reach a place of enlightenment in due time. Be proud, be bold, be confident, but do not let your ego or these glamours take over and push you in a certain direction. Be in control; recognize these glamours and release them.

Before I continue with my questions, I'd like to ask about yesterday's experience with our friend who is a healer. Do you have any comments regarding Damiana's presence at this event?

Everything is mapped out as Damiana heads down this path, and the connections, as we've said in the past, are unfolding as they should. This experience was set up for Damiana for encouragement and inspiration, and we think we achieved that goal quite well. Your friend is one of the many older souls working on their mission. He showed Damiana some of her potential in the near future and another one of the many gifts that she can experience and work with. We are quite pleased at how excited and encouraged Damiana has become.

Please talk about the aura. Does it truly exist? Can we train ourselves to see it and use it to heal?

Indeed. The aura is energy illuminating through the human body. It is often related to your energy centers, your chakras, expressed in different colors. These colors may denote something different for each individual; there's not one set interpretation. For example, red doesn't necessarily mean pain or ailment, although it could for certain individuals. Therefore, realizing and seeing these colors, finding your own interpretations, working with your own guides on these experiences, is most important. You can train yourself to become conscious of the aura with intent and focus. You can train yourself to see and work with the aura for healing purposes.

Is it best to actually focus on the aura or would it be better to try perceiving it from a different state of awareness?

Both. You are focusing on that person's energy. However, putting yourself into a higher consciousness and making a connection with your guides and their guides can help you perceive and interpret what you see when focusing on the aura.

What is love? Where does it come from? Does love have its own objective reality or existence outside of living beings?

Love is a constant; it exists in every corner of the universe. It is God. It is you. It is me. Love is everything. In human, physical form you experience love through relationships, through the connections you make and through sexual encounters. Humanity often feels the need to experience and physicalize the expression of love, which often comes out through sexual means. Love, though, flows through every inch of your body. Feel the love that flows through you; it is higher existence operating. In everyday activities find love for every being, everyone you come in touch with — your best friend and your greatest enemy. Finding that love, reaching that higher place, is quite a goal to set for yourself, for you will experience the love that you wish to share with everyone else.

What is the difference between Love and Light?

These are mostly terms for the Earth experience, but both run through you and create your very being, your very soul. Light sparks from the Godhead creating the individual soul. It is your connection with your higher Self and *All That Is*. Love radiates from Light. It's a higher expression creating a better world. It's a goal to reach for that already exists within you.

I think of Light as illumination in terms of increased consciousness. I don't think of it as a source of light on the physical plane the way that the Sun illuminates the Earth. Could you speak about Light as a consciousness-bearing influence?

Indeed. There are forms of Light beyond human comprehension. It is not like your Sun or electricity or candlelight. It is a Light that burns within each and every soul connected to higher consciousness. It is the very spark that creates your very being. It is your connection to God and *All That Is*. Light is very much higher consciousness.

Is there a difference between objective and subjective reality? Is this similar to universal constants versus personal belief systems?

Indeed. Having an objective viewpoint of your reality is subjective to each individual. Being objective in your existence as a human is important, realizing that truths and beliefs can overlap but aren't always the same. Try your best to find those truths and live your life to the utmost potential and highest plane possible.

Do most humans think they're being objective when they truly are being subjective?

Indeed, quite often. But we are not going to judge who is objective or subjective. Each being on their path is discovering and creating their reality every day, and so those beliefs and their reality might be correct for what they need right now in their life. At a certain point outside of karma we start reaching a place of service. It then becomes much more important to look at the world objectively.

By looking at the world "objectively" do you mean what is real in terms of universal constants?

Indeed. Living and being those constants so as to create by example.

What is humor? Why do people laugh? Do all beings experience humor in some form?

No. There are some extraterrestrials that do not experience humor or laughter. This emotion is beyond their compre-hension. Laughter is a form of love physicalized and is highly important for the human experience. Spreading humor and love and laughter creates relationships and connections on your planet. It is a higher form of vibration, so continue laughing, being silly, and having a good time. It's important for your vibrations.

That's good to hear because many people live their lives very seriously on this planet.

They are having their experiences for their path, but laughter is always a great way to reach higher vibrations.

When did language originate? Is speech sacred?

The *connections* that can be made through the use of language are sacred. However, we find that so much gets lost in language communication. Actually, body movement and intent are even more important forms of communication that often go unnoticed. Language began to develop on your planet at the end of Lemuria. Before that, they communicated in ethereal bodies in a much more telepathic way. As Atlantis and Egypt started to prevail and physical bodies were being used much more frequently, language began to develop for each culture. Since then, it has continued expanding into the many different languages that your planet shares today. Having these separate languages on your planet, while quite diverse, creates somewhat of a separation. Finding a global language would benefit humanity, opening up so many avenues for free-flowing communication, new ideas and developments.

Was it part of the greater plan that several languages would eventually develop or was this unintentional?

As many different cultures developed and spread out across the globe, each sect began to develop their own language within their society. Now that your world has become globalized, it's important to include more human beings, so finding a way to create a universal, global language for humanity would benefit you greatly.

Was there any type of language communication such as grunting prior to the end of the Lemurian civilization?

Yes, there was communication through body language and intent. There were vocal cords that had not developed yet to what you experience today. So, yes, there were grunting and growling noises, but communication was mostly through body language. Over time, the vocal cords developed into the dynamic that you experience today.

What is space? Are enlightened beings ever free from the constraints of space the way in which they can be free from the limitations of time?

Indeed. On the astral plane, time and space are concepts that do not apply. They are not necessary; you can experience anything you wish to experience. There are no limitations like on your planet. You can move freely into any experience. There is no space to create time. Time and space go hand-in-hand on the Earth plane. This is not so on the astral plane.

I assume that the fundamental laws such as the constants that you speak of also operate in the astral world. They must establish some kind of a framework. In that regard, can we consider them a type of limitation?

You could, but they are very different than the limitations you experience on your planet. It is a bit difficult for you to understand from the human perspective. We would not consider them limitations but just the universal constants.

Do thoughts have form? Can they be perceived as streams of energy or by the third eye?

Absolutely. Every thought, idea, or action; absolutely everything that you think or will; your imagination; all of these have form and energy. They all go out into the universe and also make up the akashic records.

Is it possible to unnaturally preserve life? Should everyone be allowed to die whenever they wish?

Absolutely. Your planet thinks of death in such a negative way. There are many planets where souls come and go quite freely from physical body to non-physical body. There were even times on *your* planet when this occurred. Death is but a change; there's nothing to fear. You are not gone; you continue moving, changing and developing. There is no reason to hold back those who are suffering on your planet. It is time for them to move on and they can feel it. It's better to release them of that pain.

Can people learn their karmic lessons without experiencing pain?

There are many ways for beings to learn their karmic lessons. Very often, however, when souls incarnate onto the Earth plane they set up these painful and suffering experiences for their karmic reasons, for they often provide the most simplistic way to release their karma.

Is the human personality like a cloak of clothing that one wears separate from the inner or true nature of one's being?

Yes and no. There is always the individual you. You are unique; you are diverse; you are your own soul. There is always the universal you as well that is connected with everyone and everything and God. Both make up who you are.

Most people seem to have an external personality or image that seems different from their true, deeper identity.

Many people on your planet wear a mask, so to speak, and they switch out these masks in different company, often for protection. They're afraid to show their true selves, who they might truly be. Fear helps disguise, so they act similar to you or what society expects of them. In that sense, there are these cloaks you speak of.

Why do people choose certain diseases? Does each disease offer specific ways to balance karma?

Often, each disease relates to their individual history. Quite often these diseases develop in later life to clean up their karmic slate before they move on or reincarnate into another body.

Is there a way for people to look at their diseases and determine what their karmic past was as a result of that disease?

Sometimes you can go back and look into your past lives and make the connections. Often, though, just experiencing the disease, getting through it, conquering it or not, will clear the karmic slate whether the individual is aware of the connection or not.

Let's consider an example where people develop emphysema or a really bad respiratory condition and have trouble breathing. Are most of these people likely to have created karma in the past, perhaps having cut off the oxygen supply of somebody else?

Indeed, it's quite possible. In that situation it's also quite possible that the pollution they've created in a past life, or in their current life, has produced this situation for them.

Were extraterrestrial bases ever established on the Moon or Mars?

There are extraterrestrials that live on the Moon and Mars, so yes.

I read from another source that Pleiadians are fifth-dimensional beings yet you have told us that you're a seventh-dimensional being. It is very confusing when we get conflicting information from different sources.

I can understand that. We are, however, seventh dimensional. For many beings, information received through the channeling process can often be tainted, manipulated, or lost in translation. We hope to come through as clear as possible and will continue working with Damiana to make the connection as strong as it possibly can be so that our information is pure and nothing is lost through translation.

Do other extraterrestrial civilizations use money as a form of trade?

Some do, some don't. Some have a bartering system, some have money similar to you, others have their own form of money, and often some like us, the Pleiadians, share our gifts with the others on our planet. We do not have a monetary system. The beings on our planet do what they are most drawn to, inspired and excited about. They are excited to share that with the other beings on our planet.

Is there a better way for humans to trade, exchange, or share resources on our planet?

Indeed. This is something you'll have to figure out in the near future. But encouraging your young ones to go towards what they're most drawn to, what they love doing — not because of monetary gain — and then sharing that with others on your planet, while providing the basic necessities of shelter, food, and healthcare for every being on your planet, what a beautiful world that could be.

Our scientists think they might have discovered a particle that travels faster than the speed of light. Can you comment on that?

Einstein's theory was quite helpful during its time, but advances in future technology will develop over time and ways for space travel, even, will be discovered.

This is very confusing to some scientists right now because Einstein's Special Theory of Relativity seems complete. I don't know if they even know where to begin to look for the holes in his theory.

Einstein's theory is complete for its time. This is very much like the example you often give of half truths, such as the Earth being flat, which it is, and being round, which it is. His Theory of Relativity was appropriate for its time. As advances in science are made, holes won't develop, per se, but new truths will grow out of them.

What causes black holes in space? Are they a concern to extra-terrestrial space travelers?

Not so much. They are energy and mass within different dimensions. From your viewpoint on the Earth, black holes seem to be sucking in and eating up your universe, but they are gateways between different dimensions.

Have you ever traveled into a black hole? Is it possible to travel into a black hole and live to talk about it?

Indeed. They are not bottomless pits as you make them out to be. They are wormholes within different dimensions.

Our scientists believe that black holes are not only sucking in a lot of matter and contain a great amount of mass, but that there are very

high temperatures in there as well, which would decimate everything that went inside.

As you continue moving into higher dimensions, new discoveries and developments will occur within your scientific fields and the mysteries of the black holes will finally be revealed, but not until you raise your vibration of the planet.

Thank you for coming through today. Do you have anything else that you'd like to share with us at this time?

I will return soon. In love and light. Many blessings.

29

Greetings, it is I, Adam. I will start today's session by discussing the purification of humanity's bloodline. What I mean by this is reaching a point in your society where there are no longer drugs and chemicals manipulating and destroying the natural form that each human is born with. You are all born perfect, exactly as you should be, but the many chemicals in your food, medications, and atmosphere are toxic and are tainting the human bloodline. So the natural antibodies and clean blood that each baby should be born with are deficient. Babies are now being born with weakened immune systems that only get weaker as they grow older and are pushed into vaccinations and pharmaceutical drugs, as well as pesticides, chemicals and hormones in your food system. It's important for the future of humanity that you become aware of these toxins that *will* put an end to the human race, and step towards a more natural and holistic way of life.

May I answer some questions today?

Yes, hi Adam. Thank you for showing up today. What is it that we can do to get from where we are today with our chemical-laden society to a more natural place?

First and foremost, your society needs to become aware that they are destroying themselves. Realize that there's a problem and together decide upon a solution, looking at the statistics and the cause and effect that constantly goes on with these chemicals, with your food supply. So many beings upon your planet are sick without actually looking at the root cause, only injecting more chemicals and poison, falling down this rabbit hole of chemical dependency. So, actually realizing and accepting that there is a problem is the first step. Then you can do proper research for oneself instead of going along with the herd and so-called experts, slowly working towards a solution.

These so-called experts are often in higher-up positions of government or industry and seem to have control over the statistical studies. They also dominate the media telling us what to believe. So there seems to be some propaganda that's going on. How do we get around that?

Yes, indeed it is time for the little person to stand up. For the next several years you will see this taking place more and more, for it is time for *everyone's* voice to be heard. Things are not working on your planet as they should be. The small minority of corporations and higher-ups are calling the shots, but there are so many more of the so-called little people who just go along because that's the way it's been, that's the way their family did it. It's time for them to stand up and have a voice, but this can only happen if they find empowerment within themselves to step outside the box of everyday societal norms. It is part of your mission, as it always has been, to make people aware of their choices on this planet. The ball is now in their court to step up, do the proper research, and make the choices needed for their family and humanity as a whole.

Yes, but I have noticed that sometimes ordinary people don't know how to do their own research or have unenlightened views. They are easily swayed by propaganda. So when they do rise up, often they rebel against their own interests or the best interests of the planet.

This is an unfortunate cause and effect sometimes. However, if you continue working on your mission and standing up for what you believe in, the cause will become clear and a chain reaction will be set in motion. Change, as we've said before, is inevitable, so certain aspects in modern society have no choice but to adapt and change. In 20, 50, or 100 years from now life as you know it will take a totally different turn of events. So continue working for what you believe in, spreading love and light, making information available to those who seek it out, and you will see the change taking place right before your eyes.

I have a question about emotions. How can people learn to control their negative emotions? For example, Damiana and I had a discussion the other day that escalated into an argument. It was disappointing for both of us. I am still mystified at how our normal conversation suddenly degenerated into a verbal clash and upsetting event. However, I think this is typical of humanity. Would you comment on this?

These strong emotions are part of the human experience and it is part of why many souls return to the planet Earth — to feel these strong emotions, to feel the strong love and even the strong hate sometimes. Noticing your negative emotions — being aware and realizing when you start to raise your temper — is the first step towards controlling it. If you continue to be aware of it, step back, look at the situation objectively, and start over. It will start to become second nature to you, and these strong, negative emotions can be a thing of the past.

It was embarrassing to have experienced that after many years of being on this spiritual path. I imagine that other light workers might feel the same way. Once they have stepped onto that path and have made a commitment to raising their lower nature into higher vibrations, it can be quite embarrassing when we find ourselves in some kind of a nonsensical argument or angry over some silly little thing.

The human experience can often be a very painful, emotional and difficult one. We are fully aware of how challenging a human experience can be, even for the most enlightened soul. Getting wrapped up in that human experience is part of the human experience and it is nothing to be embarrassed about. However, being aware of it and looking for a higher path in the future so you don't get to that place again, is in your best interest for your line of work.

The following day after we had our argument, Damiana and I both apologized and forgave each other. It felt emotionally cleansing to do that. Please speak about apologies and forgiveness.

Forgiveness is essential for holy enlightenment, not only to forgive others but to forgive yourself as well for anything that you feel you might have done wrong to yourself or others in the past. Being aware and acknowledging your mistakes or past incidences — acknowledging them and letting them go — is cleansing and healing both for yourself and those whom you apologize to and forgive.

Damiana had a very intense experience the other evening. After she had gone to sleep, she felt a strong presence next to her. This energy force was very powerful. Then she heard a voice say, "It's time!" After that, she astral-traveled to her brother and saw his past lives and where he was going to be in the future. She had some other adventures as well. It was a very profound experience for her. Can you talk about that?

Indeed. As we continue back down a path that Damiana has taken during many lifetimes, we are giving back some of the power that she has forgotten she's had with her all along. We see a very dynamic future for Damiana in this lifetime, and as we creep forward we are slowly testing the water, so to speak, to see where she's at, what she can handle, and how we should proceed. The experience was a very powerful one for Damiana and it will happen again for her. However, she still has some maturing and developing to do, so for now we will continue coming in our usual manner.

Please explain once again how it is possible for a soul to be "more evolved" or "less evolved" when a soul itself is all-knowing?

A soul is not more or less evolved. However, it could have had more physical experiences than other souls. So, in that sense you often define it as an older or younger soul, but in the astral plane the soul is *all that is* with *All That Is* and is no more or no less all-knowing.

I have a follow-up question from an earlier session regarding evolution of the spirit. You said that spirit manifested in many different forms starting out as vegetation, bacteria, animal, and then human. However, scientists believe that bacteria came before plants. Did vegetation come first before bacteria or did bacteria come before vegetation?

It is our understanding that vegetation came before bacteria developed on your planet. The planet Earth stood alone for quite some time with only vegetation, before bacteria, starting in your oceans and waters, began to develop.

I thought that plants need some kind of an insect life to pollinate them.

Not necessarily. There is cross pollination through wind and weather patterns that can develop, and many millions of years ago many of the plants that were on your planet were entirely different than the plants that exist today.

Clearly what you're teaching here is in contrast to our planet's agreed upon scientific knowledge in this field. Is that true?

There are some aspects of your scientific history that are still lost over time and some of the evidence that goes along with these theories can be confusing in an overall time frame.

If it's okay with you, I'd like to revisit the topic of religion again.

Indeed.

I'd like for you to make a few comments about some of the major religions of the world. Let's start with Buddhism.

Buddhism was never meant to be a religion on your planet, but more a way of life — living your life in a way that respects others, yourself, and *All That Is*. All of the religions have many similarities. It's this slight notion that the soul has remembering existence beyond its physical form. And so, while religions go by different names, they all have certain values and virtues that show up in each one.

Please speak about Hinduism.

Hinduism has many spiritual teachings that are following along with truths of the universe, like karma and reincarnation, concepts and constants that we've spoken of in the past. Many starseeds or more advanced souls reincarnate into this religion for it follows those guidelines that they often associate with in soul form.

Please talk about Catholicism.

The Catholic religion has been manipulated from its original form over many years. Jesus Christ never planned it to be the way that it is in modern society. His focus was on love, doing unto others as you would like them to do unto you, and empowering each individual to recognize the oneness that they have with *All That Is*. Much of this has been changed to work for individual ideas. Sticking to those root values and just living your life in a loving, holy way would suit an individual best.

Please discuss Judaism, the Jewish religion.

Judaism, one of the oldest religions on your planet, is connected to a higher power, but it can be rather traditional, and when sticking to these traditions it often excludes new ideas and concepts that can benefit an individual.

Please discuss Islam, the Muslim religion.

Islam is also a rather traditional religion that can be stuck in its ways. Once again, when you're stuck in this box it's hard to accept new, revolutionary ideas that can benefit humanity. Realizing that you're confined to this box within this religion — whether it is Islam, Judaism, or Christianity — you can step outside that box after you're aware of it, opening up to new ideas. While you still may want to practice your own individual beliefs in that higher power and way of life, accepting new concepts and other ideas can help navigate a new way to finding balance and understanding with others around you.

How do different religions of the world compare to the concept of spiritual awareness?

Many of them are stuck in this box that we've spoken of. True spirituality and awareness are about opening up and looking at all ideas, all concepts — sometimes taking them with a grain of salt — and finding *your* spirit and soul. Going within and finding what works for you is the most appropriate way to find spirit.

What do you think about religious rituals?

Some rituals, while age-old, can often harm other beings on your planet. You can come to an understanding and realization that in modern society this is not necessary, that true spirituality can be found within. The answers are *all* there for your asking. So, if you can practice these rituals in a way where you are not harming yourself or others, and if they awaken you with a relevant path to your divine self, then they can be appropriate.

What's the difference between a religion and a cult?

Mostly these are just names. Cults are often considered anti-religion, not always believing in a higher power or divine self. Most religions believe in a higher Self or a higher power and that is not always necessary within a cult.

Are religious holy books truly holy?

Anything can be holy to an individual if you make it that way. If it speaks to the soul, then you can find holy divinity within it.

Is there such a thing as a holy war?

Again, if it speaks to the soul. I'm not sure that I've seen a war that does that, but perhaps to certain individuals it has.

Are some areas of the planet more sacred than others?

If an individual finds an area where they can discover their higher power or God or themselves, then yes, there are places that each individual can look upon as sacred. Your whole planet is a sacred location.

So it's not as though one place is objectively sacred and another place is objectively less sacred. This sacred connotation is based upon an individual's own beliefs. Is that correct?

Indeed.

Do energy vortexes really exist? If so, what causes them?

There are indeed places on your planet and throughout the universe that are gateways to other dimensions and worlds where many spiritual beings have been. Individuals can often pick up on these vibrations and feel that higher energy.

Who was Pythagoras? Was he an advanced being from another world?

Pythagoras was an advanced soul who had been to your planet, and others, many times. He studied mathematics of the universe including many different patterns, dimensions, and concepts. You could call him a universal mathematician forever looking for answers to the entire makeup of *All That Is*.

Where is Plato today?

Plato is living on the other side and can be channeled. He is forever the philosopher, helping many philosophers on your planet with inspiration and answers.

You called Pythagoras a universal mathematician. Here on the Earth, how advanced is our current understanding of mathematics?

There are some astrophysicists and quantum physicists that have gotten very close to higher mathematics. However, mathematics, which represents patterns of the universe, can be found in everything — *All That Is*. Therefore, mathematics can reach nearly infinite levels. At your current history on your planet it is still rather novice.

You and Naor have recommended tapping into the Earth's magnetic fields and increasing our development of solar power. What are some other renewable energy sources that you would recommend?

There is energy within each individual that can be tapped into. There is wind energy and weather energy, working with your weather patterns. There is energy from your plants, plant life, that can be worked with as well. We recommend looking into the individual being's energy, for you have an infinite supply of this energy.

What type of scientist would be best equipped to understand and discover how to utilize this energy within each of us?

Young scientists and new generations of scientists, ones willing to step outside the box using their imagination to delve into brand new ideas and concepts, scientists that aren't trying to stick to old fields and old ideas. This is true in all aspects of different occupations and concepts on your planet.

Do you think that a psychologist or biologist would be more likely to discover this energy?

What we are saying is none of those. It will require a brand new field created from a brand new scientist. These old boxes that you put individuals into — biologists, psychologists, chemists — are all boxes with labels. We are saying that brand new scientists who *won't* go into those boxes, who refuse to go into those boxes, who are working towards a better world, a better future, a new Earth, they are the ones equipped to make these changes.

If some extraterrestrials do not experience emotions, are they able to appreciate a pretty landscape or object of beauty?

Not in the way that you are able to appreciate beauty. They look at a pretty picture or member of the opposite sex from a different point of view. In an opposite mate they might find beauty in big hips or an asymmetrical face. In a picture, beauty might be something that mathematically adds up to most realistic or perfect, but they do not see beauty in the sense that you as a human see beauty.

Do you have recommendations on how to help our autistic children?

Your autistic children need to be cherished for they are often experiencing and tuned into certain aspects that most of humanity overlooks. You can appreciate them, helping them learn, grow and discover other parts of humanity, while also focusing on what they are most interested in and often quite developed at.

Autistic children are often very difficult to raise; it's a very complicated and emotional experience for the parents. Are there any treatment protocols that you can recommend so that these children and their parents can live less painful and difficult lives?

These experiences that both the parent and the autistic child are going through are often karmic. However, some solace can be found by always approaching any situation with love and understanding, working with the child instead of against them, paying attention to what sets them off, where they find comfort, and working with what's most appropriate for that child and the parent.

What is some of the karma that these parents are bearing? They expected a healthy child and ended up with a lifetime of caring for a very difficult child. It's also painful for the parents to see their children go through these experiences.

There are all different types of karmic past that the individual could have. Perhaps they have neglected children in the past or have hurt others or have been difficult to deal with in past lives. This is some of the karma they may be dealing with.

In an earlier session it was stated that scientists are aware of some cures that plants offer but are keeping these cures hidden. Why would scientists keep plant cures hidden?

Sometimes they use these plants for their own benefit but not as a global, useful way to help humanity. Curing many of these diseases would end their profitable careers. Continuing these diseases maintains the corporate greed.

It sounds like you're saying that some industries in the field of traditional healthcare may have scientists on their payroll who found cures to some diseases but they are suppressing that information because it allows them to make a greater profit with other treatments.

Indeed. They enjoy controlling your society. They manipulate the use of known cures or continue the disease because they like holding your life in their hands.

Do they actually like holding our lives in their hands or do they do this because it enables them to make more money?

Both. It's a cycle between money, power and manipulation.

Dr. Steven Greer established the "Disclosure Project." He is trying to make people aware of a shadow government that exists beside the legitimate government and is suppressing information about extraterrestrial existence. Can you speak about this?

Indeed. He is one of the individuals working physically to bring forth the truth behind many of the cover-ups on your planet. As we said before, there are many extraterrestrials that have visited your planet and have been working with your government. He will continue trying to bring forth this information to the masses as it is important in that form as well as in this form that we have taken on.

Thank you very much for coming through. We really appreciate it. Is there anything else you'd like to share with us before we end today's session?

Thank you. Things will continue progressing as they should and will develop further along. Many blessings. In love and light.

Forgiveness is essential for holy enlightenment, not only to forgive others but to forgive yourself as well for anything that you feel you might have done wrong to yourself or others in the past. Acknowledging your mistakes and letting them go is cleansing and healing both for yourself and those whom you apologize to and forgive.

30

How to get from point A to point B, recognizing that the Earth has many problems at this time. How to develop a list, research those problems, and open up to a new planet. While these issues are planetary and quite large, and require quite a lot of time and money to fix, it is in everyone's best interest to take care of them — a global to-do list.

First of all, identify and organize, in urgency, what's most important and needs to be fixed first. Put together a list of what's most important — poverty, world hunger, economic issues — much like your weekend to-do list: cleaning the house, fixing some shutters, gardening. While some of them might be more difficult, you can put them in a list that is most urgent and important for change and then go to work on them.

Take world hunger, for example. Where do you begin? There are a lot of sub-issues with this category, such as genetically modified foods. Is this a pro or a con? Jungles that are destroyed for cattle is another sub-issue. Most inhabitants on Earth eat insects. However, for some reason most English-speaking beings on your planet avoid this (and are disgusted by it). But did you know that cattle cost millions of dollars to feed and farm, destroy your planet to raise, and only produce 18 percent protein with 18 percent fat, while insects eat natural food — fruits, vegetables, grass — cost very little to raise, and produce 30 percent protein and only 6 percent fat?

Looking at these alternatives and different ways of life on your planet could help people come together to raise new ideas and consciousness about how you could globally feed everyone and take care of your planet. Healthcare, shelter, and global warming all need to be placed on the list and looked at (for as we've said before, you're at a tipping point with global warming). It's time for the people of planet Earth to look at these issues and stop pushing them under the rug. Let them surface, organize them, and go to work. The ball is in your court.

It is I, Adam. May I answer some questions today?

Yes, hi Adam. Thank you for that nice dissertation on prioritizing our problems here on the Earth. Of course, as you know, it's not an easy task to get people to agree not only on what the problems are, but on how to go about solving them because many people will resist. For example, large corporations that are invested in genetically modified foods would resist any kind of a call for doing away with them if that's what the people decided was necessary for an enlightened planet.

As you are seeing, the voice of the people — the large percentage — is slowly developing, is starting to take place. Don't underestimate the power of the people to make change. Do your part — make your change — and a chain reaction will occur around you. Come together, hearing the pros and cons of different situations and ideas on how to help work and save the planet. Although large corporations may not agree on health issues, they might propose that perhaps genetically modified foods could help feed more of the people. And feeding more of the people is a mutual starting point where you both agree that there needs to be change. Start at these points of interest putting everything on the table, all the different ideas, ones that maybe you do or don't agree with, looking at all the pros and cons and how it's in the best interest of the people and the planet Earth to create that change.

Did you just suggest that genetically modified foods may be a positive option to feeding people on the planet?

It is *an* option and it is up to your planet to look at the pros and cons of *all* the options.

We're having a difficult time in our country just getting genetically modified foods labeled so that the people have a choice as to whether or not they even want them in their diet.

Indeed. Bringing forth these issues, making them known and letting the people have a voice and have those choices is important, as many of your choices are being taken away without your awareness. Be aware, recognize, and come together for an alternative way of life.

Damiana and I just finished watching a video of the Disclosure Project, where several people in positions of high responsibility, with top-secret clearance, spoke about their experiences with UFOs and extraterrestrials. Can you comment on this?

Indeed. This is one of those issues that is hidden right beneath your nose. The shadow government, which we've spoken of before, is keeping this technology for military use when much of it could be put to global benefit and understanding, to help you come to new energy resources and stop destroying your planet. Working from all different angles will bring forth the truth. Steven Greer is doing his part to disclose the truth. It is very important that everyone works at their mission and their goal, and all the puzzle pieces will come together.

Yesterday, Damiana had an experience that was a little bit startling. It was similar to the experience she had the other day when she was sleeping. We started to meditate and she was planning on doing a reading for somebody when she felt very intense energy on her head. She thought that if she submitted to that energy she would not be able to return or perhaps she would die. Can you comment on that?

Indeed. As we've said before, we are slowly testing the water, so to speak, getting Damiana comfortable returning to her power in her field of work. We are just at the tip of the iceberg with her energy and line of work. And so, as Damiana continues down this path we will continue pushing the limits and testing the boundaries until she reaches and returns to a comfort level that she's had in the past. We will continue giving samples and testing. Eventually, it will become second nature and she'll fall into her craft. The energy and the feelings are new and unusual to her at this time, so she's weary and nervous, which is normal.

She'll become more comfortable and get used to it as it becomes more frequent, as it will.

The other day you said that Damiana's guides are giving her back some of her power. What did you mean?

We are not giving her back her power; *she* is giving herself permission to use that higher power again. It is there and has been with her this whole life and all her lives. As she's developing and growing, she's slowly letting more of that power express itself and grow. It is always with her but would be overwhelming and too much if it came all at once.

Is this idea about Damiana receiving back her power associated with an agreement before she came onto the planet?

Indeed, it is a mutual agreement circle with all of us as she slowly gets back her power.

What is the actual energy that she's experiencing? It's clearly an objective experience that she's having.

It is her own energy. It is *extremely* strong and powerful, as is *every* individual's energy, and it has the utmost potential for change, growth, and universal fuel. It is limitless. She has an infinite amount of it, as do you and others. Damiana is slowly letting it come back to power.

I have a few follow-up questions to earlier sessions that we've had. Are you open to answering them?

Indeed.

The other day, Damiana traveled with her third eye to another planet where they harnessed lightning from electrical storms for use as an energy source. Is this a viable alternative energy source here on the Earth?

Absolutely, if you get enough lightning storms. The weather has energy sources. The wind, solar, lightning, and rain all have natural energy sources that can fuel and rejuvenate your planet.

You have already somewhat tapped into solar and wind, but there is so much more where that came from. Putting more time and research into these alternative energy sources would benefit your planet greatly.

What is the difference between an out-of-body experience and traveling, or perceiving, with one's third eye?

There are different levels of out-of-body experiences. When you travel in your dreams, this is very similar to traveling with your third eye. Your consciousness can leave the body or you can bring forth different experiences to your consciousness. There are also experiences, like near-death experiences that people have had, where they have left their body and will sometimes return, or not, at the end of life. This is not just the consciousness leaving, but the whole being — soul, mind, consciousness — all choosing that it's time to leave and go a different way.

In an earlier session there seemed to be a distinction being made between Damiana actually traveling somewhere versus her bringing those experiences to her consciousness in the here and now.

Indeed, this is very similar, her consciousness going somewhere or bringing forth those experiences to her consciousness. In order for your benefit to have Damiana tell you about those experiences in present time, and to be able to hear her, she must bring forth those experiences to her consciousness. However, she can — and does every night — let her consciousness go and travel as it wishes.

Will she be able to leave her body, go somewhere in real time and observe events happening on the physical planet, then return to her body and describe those events that she perceived from a great distance?

With time and purpose, yes, Damiana could eventually accomplish that.

I have a question about the evolution of planets. Did your Pleiadian sister planets raise their vibration from the third to the seventh dimensions over time or were they always seventh-dimensional planets?

Oh, no. We, too, have traveled through different dimensions. We were, at one point, third-dimensional beings such as yourselves. Over time, the natural evolution of planets and beings naturally gravitates towards higher dimensions, and with conscious work of the beings on the planet you can reach these higher levels.

Do the Earth and other planets have DNA or is it only found in humans and other living organisms? Do angels and ascended masters have DNA?

Physical bodies carry DNA, so when a being incarnates, whether it is human, animal, or extraterrestrial, DNA will be found — different DNA, different strands, different types. Non-physical beings, such as angels and ascended masters, do not carry DNA with them.

Are you a non-physical being?

I have a physical body on my planet. We have developed to a point where we can easily go back and forth from physical to non-physical, but we do have physical bodies.

Is the Earth a physical organism or a mineral? Is there a great being that actually occupies the Earth? Does it have any kind of DNA?

There is a presence of Mother Earth, as you call her. There is no DNA that is similar to humanity's within Mother Earth, but there are certain minerals that make up and create the celestial body that is unique to her.

How did karma first get started? How did bad karma originate?

You identify it as bad. As we have said before, these are labels which you have given it. Karma exists without limitations of time. While time on your planet is linear, karma is a circle; there is no beginning or end. It is connected in every sense.

Please comment on the relationship between corporations and labor unions.

This is one of the many issues that your planet will have to come to terms with, these corporations that are making all the money for the leaders to live the high life, corrupt and greedy, while the people who are doing the hard work are often living close to poverty. It is time for the labor unions to step up and have a voice, to come forth and realize that they hold the power, not the corporations.

Was it not the leaders of the corporations who had the ingenuity and took the risks to initiate and grow their businesses?

Indeed, and now it's time for the balance of power to shift, for it is too over-the-top unbalanced right now. So it is time for the followers to stand up for themselves and become leaders.

Please talk more about the passions that people have, what makes them happy and how they can find their true purpose.

Passion is decided before incarnation, what makes them happy and what their goals and path will be in that individual life. Take time to experience different careers and ways of life. Discover what truly raises your individual vibration, truly makes you happy, and then alter everything in your life to live that passion. Everyone has the potential and opportunity to be and live their passion.

When people start to accomplish their true passion or their true purpose, is this a type of self-actualization?

Indeed, absolutely. When you lay the blueprints for a new planet, setting it up so that it caters to these individuals trying out and discovering their passion — not catering to more greed and monetary needs — what truly makes each individual happy will create a more satisfying and livable planet for everyone.

We have a group meditation planned for later this week and we're very much looking forward to it. Do you have any comments on that upcoming experience?

Indeed. These will continue and grow; more individuals will join you as we make the connections. Don't take these very beginning meditations too seriously. It's a "getting to know you" process, getting to feel each other's energy and get used to the new dynamic. The more important and higher level of channeling that Damiana will begin to do will develop on its own at its own pace. So just enjoy the meditations, feeling each other's energy, getting to know everyone.

Thank you very much. Do you have anything else you'd like to share with us before we end today's session?

Continue doing your meditations. Don't underestimate the power and work being done behind the scenes when we aren't coming through. We will be back soon, though, and are always with you. Many blessings. In love and light.

31

Good day, it is I, Ilana. Can I shed some light and answer some questions for you today?

Yes, hi Ilana. I have a few questions. Some of them are follow-ups, but not all of them are. Please discuss the internet. Did the idea for the internet originate from extraterrestrials?

Indeed. This is some of the technology that was developed through connections made with different extraterrestrial groups. This is one of the few technologies that has been shared with the masses. There are many others that your government has kept hidden and is still working on and developing for their own personal use. Eventually this will become clearer as these technologies are developed out into the future.

I thought that the internet was originally developed for the military.

Indeed. Eventually the connection out to the public was made, realizing the potential it had for a global connection on your planet.

WikiLeaks is an organization that gained access to sensitive communication between top officials of several different nations. They released that information on the internet. Do you think this is positive or potentially destructive?

We think it just is. The more that the masses know, the more potential there is for growth. Keeping anything hidden in the dark creates a box in which it has no room to grow, develop, or come clean — even certain aspects that are potentially dangerous or scary to the public. If you know about it, it is easier to deal with, work around, and find a solution. So we think that the more that leaks and secrets get out so that the masses can take the best route to solving problems is in your best interest.

Some of the information that was leaked was between ambassadors of different nations. These were private communications. Do nations have a right to communicate with other nations with an understanding that their dialogue is private?

Of course they have the right to. But, again, this is one of the very reasons that we, the Pleiadians, have switched to a non-vocal form of communication. Telepathy is open to anyone, anywhere. We have no secrets. When humanity reaches this point of trust and understanding, with a high enough vibration without fear, then there will be no reason for these secret dialogues to take place. Open communication will be the universal road to brotherhood.

Are oxygen and water necessary to sustain extraterrestrial life?

Certain extraterrestrial life, but no. There are many different types of extraterrestrial life in all different forms. Oxygen and air are not necessarily needed for all of them.

Why do animals have to kill other animals in order to eat?

This is, as you call it on your planet, the circle of life. *All* things on your planet have a purpose and a point. For example, the deer is doing its part. It's living its life, eating grass, and is aware that the lion will kill it. This is part of its life as a deer and the circle of life, the circle of karma, and the circle of celestial growth.

Do animals on Pleiades kill other animals in order to eat?

Indeed. We, too, have a circle of life. And there is quite an understanding and a balance within our nature. If the lions do not kill the deer, the deer would overpopulate and create an imbalance within nature. So there is a perfect balance with each and every animal, plant, and insect.

Speaking of insects, do you think it's a good idea for humans to include them in their diets? Many cultures have already added insects to their diets, but do you think that we could be eating even more insects?

Indeed. This is something that humanity will have to look at. However, we think that with the abundance of insects on your planet, and the abundance of beings who are underfed, and the immense loss of jungles and plant life to raise cattle — which are being pumped full of chemicals that aren't even helping the health of humanity, but are instead contributing to obesity and other diseases — that insects, which are high in protein and low in fat, would be a great way to sustain human life.

Would this alter the web of life?

It would change it, but with some restraint — not mass producing insects, pumping them full of chemicals and trying to alter their natural growth — you could create a fine balance in the circle of life.

What do you think of our boxing matches on the Earth where two men battle each other with their fists?

Natural testosterone levels within men create a high need for competition, which we think is fine and healthy when two parties agree and the competition is not ill-intended or meant to hurt each other to the point of pain or destruction, for there is a natural testosterone level that is always being reproduced. So a natural release of this energy, we think, is fine, so that men are not going out and hurting others.

What does mathematics look like on Pleiades? Do you calculate math on computers or in your head? Do you use symbols that are similar to our numbers?

Indeed. Mathematics is found throughout the universe. It represents the patterns and symbols of *All That Is*. These connections are made and found in nature, science, everything in the universe. Our mathematics, while similar to yours, is more developed with higher patterns and more consciousness of the mathematics found in nature. Our technology does indeed do calculations for us. But we also like to keep our brains sharp, so we try to keep up with the mathematics of the time. We do not have school systems like you do, so our children, unless drawn to and naturally interested in the mathematics of nature, do not learn the same mathematics that you do on your planet. They do, however, realize and recognize the connections and patterns shown by example in everyday life.

Damiana did a reading the other day and the woman's spiritual guide told her there are no wrong choices. Please elaborate on this idea.

Again, right and wrong are labels upon your planet. So telling this woman that she has no wrong choice lets her know that there are consequences for every action, and how you look at those consequences determines whether they are positive or negative. If you *always* look at a consequence and find the positive energy in *every* interaction, there will be no wrong choices.

There may be no wrong choices, but are some choices better than others?

That is up to the individual's opinion.

I've always admired Paramahansa Yogananda, the East Indian teacher who taught meditation to Westerners and established the Self-Realization Fellowship. Where is Yogananda today?

Yogananda has ascended and is working as a master with individuals through channelings. You can connect with him through meditation and channeling, as he works as a guide for many beings on your planet.

Please comment on music. What do Pleiadians think about our music on the Earth?

Music is a form of vibration, and while you have many different forms of music on your planet, you have barely tapped into the diverse vibrational tones yet to be discovered that can create an array of unique types of music on your planet.

Damiana had a dream experience the other day that was disturbing to her. She felt like she had woken up a couple of times in her room and yet she was still dreaming or in an in-between state of some sort. She didn't seem to be able to truly wake herself up out of this dream state. She felt paralyzed. Can you comment on this?

Indeed. Damiana's soul was still out exploring, yet part of her consciousness was back in her room ready to wake up. But without her soul in her body, her body was in fact paralyzed, so to speak, and she could not move or get up or control her body without the return of her soul. This is an in-between state where she is in deep REM sleep but still gone dreaming.

Where was her soul?

It was in the astral plane exploring. Her consciousness was focused in the room, however.

Well, that's my short list of questions for today. Do you have any additional comments?

Everything is developing as it should. Some of these periods will move forward quite rapidly, so when there is a lull it sometimes feels like a plateau. These adjustment periods are just as important as the rapidly moving forward periods, so do not look down on them as any less. Continue eagerly working on the book, for we are quite excited about this publication. Continue raising your vibrations and looking forward to each day and the new horizon with love, understanding and compassion for your brother and sister, with a smile on your face and love in your heart. I bid you good day. In love and light.

Passion is decided before incarnation. Discover what truly raises your individual vibration, truly makes you happy, and then alter everything in your life to live that passion.

32

Good day, it is I, Naor. Please, Neil, hold on to your questions, for they will be needed in the future, but right now I would like to bring this book full circle. I wish to thank the readers — as well as Neil, Susanne and Damiana, my Earth family that I hope to work with again in the future. We have been very pleased with our exchanges over time and hope that our message will get out there and be taken to heart. The Earth is in great need of healers, lovers, and a new beginning.

If you take away only one thing from this book, please understand this: *love conquers all*. It always has and always will. Feel that love radiate from within you, sharing it with everyone you come into contact with.

Find within yourself your own inner strength and wisdom. It will bring answers that are beyond *our* light and growth. Your *own* higher Self knows all. Trust it, look to it, and believe in your Self. Start creating that change. The time is now.

Good morning. It is I, Adam. I would like to start off the conclusion to our project by thanking my Earth family: Neil, Susanne, Damiana, and Jeremiah. Your discipline and dedication to this project has truly shown through and brought honor to myself and the many, many beings eager to make contact and help humanity, leading the way into a promising and beautiful new future.

The potential that each individual has to create change is above and beyond anything that any of us can bring down and give to you. The power that you hold within yourself has so much potential; bring it forth.

Choosing to incarnate on the planet Earth at this time in Earth's history is commendable. Every single human being is working out one of the most difficult experiences in the universe. Realize that and be proud of being human. It is not an easy experience, and each and every one of you is at the top of your class.

Your Mother Earth is screaming for your attention now. The climate is changing, the ice caps are melting, the Great Barrier Reef is being bleached; these are all nudges and pleas and begs from your Mother Earth to pay attention to her. It is each and everyone's duty as an Earthling, as a human being. Take heed and do your part. It's time now to step outside of yourself joining with other souls to help create a beautiful tomorrow for your children so that they, too, can experience the wonder and magic of the Earth.

Push fear to the wayside and let love illuminate the path. Love is the answer and the key to any growth and power for change. Set a shining example of the potential that each and every individual holds within. Reach deep into your heart and pull forth a bright, beautiful new Earth.

Many blessings. In love and light.

Index

Twinkle in the Eve

When God declared "Let there be light!"
He took the world by storm.
His plan was to unveil the night,
Then give it shape and form.

Of course, He had some space to fill
For all was stark and vast.
So with a mighty burst of will
He birthed the ancient past.

It started with a fertile thought
Transmuting force to mass.
Then everything evolved from naught
When He burped out some gas!

Great stars emerged to fill the void
While planets traveled round.
But if God could become annoyed
At one new breeding ground

Where life appeared to creep and crawl
From this to that to man,
And living things just seem to brawl
Throughout their mortal span

It would be Earth, your cherished globe
Where free-will sets your fate,
And few indeed are apt to probe
The worlds they re-create.

So search within to find the force
Behind the mass you are.
It is the power of your source;
The light of your own star.

You are a 'Sun of God' on clay
And make what you conceive,
So radiate throughout the day
And twinkle in the eve.

—NZM

Summon the Light

Damiana Sage Miller receives messages from ascended masters, angels, archangels, benevolent extraterrestrials, and other beings of Light. For more information, visit her website:

www.SummonTheLight.com

Purchasing Information

Additional copies of *Ambassadors Between Worlds: Intergalactic Gateway to a New Earth* (ISBN: 978-1881217381) may be purchased directly from *New Atlantean Press*. Call 505-983-1856. Or send $15.95 (in U.S. funds), plus $5.00 shipping, to:

New Atlantean Press
PO Box 9638
Santa Fe, NM 87504
505-983-1856 (Telephone & Fax)
Email: think@thinkchoice.com

This book is also available at many fine bookstores:
ISBN: 978-1881217381

Bookstores/Libraries/Retail Buyers: Order from Midpoint, Baker &Taylor, Ingram, New Leaf, or New Atlantean Press.

Starseeds and other Non-Storefront Buyers: Take a 40% discount with the purchase of 5 or more copies (multiply the total cost of purchases x .60). Please add 9% ($5.00 minimum) for shipping. *Larger discounts are available.*

Shipping: Please add 9% ($5.00 minimum) for shipping. Allow 1-3 weeks for your order to arrive, or include $2.00 extra for priority air mail shipping. **Foreign orders** should email us for rates: think@thinkchoice.com

Also Available from New Atlantean Press

Holy Christ Revealed: The True Life of Jesus, Including Details of His Birth, Teen Years and Spiritual Mission (ISBN: 1-881217337). A complete and accurate record of the words and deeds of Jesus. Includes intimate details surrounding his birth, early childhood, teen years and spiritual mission. In this phenomenal book, you will read about the monks, wise men, masters and prophets that Jesus visited, learned from and taught, during his journeys through India, Tibet, Persia, Greece and Egypt prior to embarking on his divine ministry. New parables, immortal wisdom and miraculous feats not recorded in the New Testament are documented in this book. From the birth of Mother Mary to the trial, crucifixion and resurrection of Jesus, your heart will open and spirit quicken as the Holy Christ is revealed. Code: HCR (192 pages) $14.95.

Gadzooks! Extraterrestrial Guide to Love, Wisdom and Happiness (ISBN: 1-881217213). Extraordinary beings from other worlds offer insight, guidance, and a lyrical blueprint for your spiritual growth. Code GAD (96 pages) $9.95.

ONLINE CATALOG: *New Atlantean Press* offers a unique selection of books on spiritual inspiration and holistic health. Visit:

www.thinkchoice.com